# Health and Well-being in Early Childhood

Janet Rose • Louise Gilbert • Val Richards

Los Angeles | London | New Delhi
Singapore | Washington DC

Los Angeles | London | New Delhi
Singapore | Washington DC

SAGE Publications Ltd
1 Oliver's Yard
55 City Road
London EC1Y 1SP

SAGE Publications Inc.
2455 Teller Road
Thousand Oaks, California 91320

SAGE Publications India Pvt Ltd
B 1/I 1 Mohan Cooperative Industrial Area
Mathura Road
New Delhi 110 044

SAGE Publications Asia-Pacific Pte Ltd
3 Church Street
#10-04 Samsung Hub
Singapore 049483

Editor: Jude Bowen
Editorial assistant: George Knowles
Production editor: Tom Bedford
Copyeditor: Peter Williams
Proofreader: Caroline Stock
Indexer: Grace Rose
Marketing manager: Dilhara Attygalle
Cover design: Wendy Scott
Typeset by: C&M Digitals (P) Ltd, Chennai, India
Printed and bound by CPI Group (UK) Ltd,
Croydon, CR0 4YY

**Library of Congress Control Number: 2015935507**

**British Library Cataloguing in Publication data**

A catalogue record for this book is available from
the British Library

ISBN 978-1-4462-8730-9
ISBN 978-1-4462-8762-0 (pbk)

At SAGE we take sustainability seriously. Most of our products are printed in the UK using FSC papers and boards.
When we print overseas we ensure sustainable papers are used as measured by the Egmont grading system.
We undertake an annual audit to monitor our sustainability.

# Health and Well-being in Early Childhood

**SAGE** was founded in 1965 by Sara Miller McCune to support the dissemination of usable knowledge by publishing innovative and high-quality research and teaching content. Today, we publish more than 850 journals, including those of more than 300 learned societies, more than 800 new books per year, and a growing range of library products including archives, data, case studies, reports, and video. SAGE remains majority-owned by our founder, and after Sara's lifetime will become owned by a charitable trust that secures our continued independence.

Los Angeles | London | New Delhi | Singapore | Washington DC

# CONTENTS

# LIST OF FIGURES
# AND TABLES

## Figures

## Tables

# ACKNOWLEDGEMENTS

We would like to thank all the practitioners and colleagues for their contributions to this book and to all the children whose stories we tell in our case studies. In particular, we'd like to thank Julia Butler, Tracey Barnett, Alison Cliffe, Licette Gus, Heidi Limbert, Linda Plowden, Rosie Pritchard, Angela Spencer and Sara Willis. In addition, we would like to thank Christopher Walker for his illustrations and Felicia Wood, Kate Cairns and Tracey Lewarne for their helpful comments during the writing of this book.

We would also like to extend our thanks to Jude Bowen, Amy Jarrold and George Knowles of Sage for their guidance and support.

# ABOUT THE AUTHORS

Dr Janet Rose is currently a Principal Lecturer and Programme Leader in Early Education at Bath Spa University. A former teacher, she has also worked in a range of early years settings, worked with children 'at risk' and ran sensory integration workshops for 0-3s for many years both in England and abroad. She has worked closely with the National College of Teaching and Learning and led training for a number of Local Authorities and professional organisations around the country. She is the author of various publications, including a co-authored book on The Role of the Adult in Early Years Settings. She is currently developing two research projects (Attachment Aware Schools and Emotion Coaching) which focus on supporting children's behaviour and well-being.

Louise Gilbert's background is in health and education having trained as a teacher and a nurse, and worked in health promotion before becoming a university Senior Lecturer in childhood with a special interest in child development and health. She has numerous publications with a focus on sustainable health and well-being. Louise has also contributed to the development of professional training programmes, delivered keynote speeches and run workshops for multidisciplinary and specialist groups working with children. With Janet Rose, she designed and delivered the first UK Emotion Coaching research project, which applied an interpersonal neurobiological approach to support sustainable, community-wide, cross-disciplinary promotion of children's well-being and resilience. She is currently writing her doctoral thesis on the research findings.

Val Richards is a Senior Lecturer at Bath Spa University. She is a member of the Education Studies department and currently leads and teaches modules on Health, Education and Behaviour, Adolescent Development, and Learning. Her main discipline is psychology, specialising in developmental psychology, adolescence, health psychology and teaching and learning. She has also taught Food and Nutrition and Childhood Studies at both Higher Education and secondary school level and was subject leader for Studies of Childhood at Bath Spa University. Her research has focused on gender-related behaviour and attitudes and, more recently, issues concerning transitions from primary to secondary school. She has recently co-edited a book on Bridging the Transition from Primary to Secondary School.

# INTRODUCTION

The significance of young children's health and well-being is well established and increasingly on the agenda of government departments and agencies worldwide. This worldwide concern for, and understanding of, childhood well-being has increased over the past decade (UNICEF, 2013a). National success is no longer considered to be exclusively defined by traditional economic indicators such as Gross Domestic Product, but should also assess societal progress by measuring well-being (Stiglitz et al., 2010). The United Nations Convention on the Rights of the Child recognises a child's right to survive and thrive, to learn and grow, to have their voices heard, and to reach their full potential. This includes addressing their health and well-being, an issue that continues to permeate not just the non-Western world, but also shows signs of regressing in the Western world (UNCRC, 1989). A recent UNICEF (2014a) report calls for more information regarding the improvement of children's health and well-being to be made available.

## What is health and well-being?

Defining health and well-being is challenging given that it may mean different things to different people in different socio-cultural contexts. It might be viewed objectively (such as via health status or household income) or subjectively (via personal perceptions of quality of life) (Statham and Chase, 2010). When considering definitions of health, we might only view health as relating to *physical* health but this does not reflect the growing evidence of how *emotional* health can affect our physical health. For example, it has been shown that mental illness and stress affect the immune system and reduce life expectancy (NIMH, 2013). Similarly, we might enjoy physical health but still not have life satisfaction or a sense of happiness due to other needs not being met, such as financial security. Therefore, being healthy includes our *mental* health and well-being. This was affirmed by the World Health Organisation back in 1948 who defined health as a 'state of complete physical, mental and social well-being' (WHO, 1948). Later, this definition was amended to accommodate the realities of achieving this objective (such as personal and social capabilities) and drew attention to the processes involved in promoting health (WHO, 1984).

When we look for definitions of well-being we can see further complexity in attempting a definition. For example, Pollard and Lee's (2002) review of well-being identifies five different domains for well-being – physical, psychological, cognitive, social and economic. In England, the National Institute for Health and Care Excellence (NICE, 2012) separates well-being into three different categories – emotional, psychological and social – and identifies a wide range of factors that ought to be considered. These aspects address factors such as being happy and confident and having good relationships with others to managing emotions and being resilient.

In relation to the early years, Laevers (1994) has characterised well-being in children as reflecting factors such as openness and receptivity, self-confidence and self-esteem, vitality, enjoyment, relaxation and inner peace and self-assurance. Laevers equates higher levels of well-being (in other words, children who display high levels of these signals) with having an increased capacity to learn and being more deeply engaged, motivated and interested in learning. This might entail being able to persist and engage with more complex and creative aspects of learning. Roberts (2010) has also created a holistic framework of well-being for early years practice which centres around having a sense of agency and a sense of belonging, recognising the determining factor played by communication and active interaction in achieving well-being, and how all this rests on a bedrock of physical well-being.

In many respects the terms health and well-being can be used interchangeably (Walker and John, 2012); for example, emotional health might also be considered the same as emotional well-being, or at least that one leads to the other. In this book, health and well-being is used as a single term *health and well-being*. Within this term, it is acknowledged that:

- they are dynamic and multi-faceted concepts;
- they involve physical, emotional and mental manifestations;
- they are processes not just products;
- that one invariably affects the other.

A *multi-dimensional perspective* is therefore needed in order to understand the meaning of health and well-being and how best to promote both. This book draws on interdisciplinary frameworks to explore what is involved in supporting young children's health and well-being – a *biopsychosocial* model, a *psychoneurobiological* model and an *ecological systems* model, all of which provide us with an evidence-base and a more robust insight into health and well-being.

# The biopsychosocial model of human development

For many years, developmental psychology has tended to dominate our understanding of how children develop. However, increased research and technological advances have introduced different ways of thinking about how different disciplines within the natural and social sciences need to work together to produce more holistic perspectives on how to support children's development. This is particularly true in relation to health and well-being as new discoveries reveal how everything affects everything else at multiple levels and in varying ways (Rutten et al., 2013). As our knowledge of the physiological, psychological, socio-logical and neurobiological components of childhood increases, traditional boundaries between different disciplines are breaking down. It is now increasingly accepted that we need to adopt what has been termed a *consilience* approach to understanding human development (Sroufe and Siegel, 2011). That is, we need to draw upon the evidence from a range of fields that reach the same conclusions and blend these insights to create a unity of knowledge and understanding about health and well-being in the early years. This includes dissolving traditional debates about nurture versus nature and recognising the *contingent and recursive* relationship between physiological, neurological and behavioural responses in order to optimise well-being (Siegel, 1999). This involves, for example, recognising the evidence that genes (*biology*) and experiences (*environment*) are indivisible, interrelated and interde-pendent with each affecting and enabling the expression and growth of the other in order to create the *psychological mind* (McCrory et al., 2010). Feldman and Eidelman have affirmed this from their research which reflects the 'dynamic interchange of biological dispositions and environmental provisions' (2009: 194). In other words, the genetic structure we are born with transacts with a range of environmental stimuli and influences, which in turn interface to create the person that we are. The National Scientific Council on the Developing Child based at Harvard University in America has confirmed that

> the biology of health explains how experiences and environmental influences 'get under the skin' and interact with genetic predispositions, which then result in various combinations of physiological adaptation and disruption that affect lifelong outcomes in learning, behavior, and both physical and mental well-being (NSCDC, 2010: 5).

In essence, they combine to create a *biopsychosocial* model of child development which correlates with the comprehensive *pyschoneurobiological* model of health and well-being on which this book is based.

## The pyschoneurobiological model of brain, body and mind

The biopsychosocial model of human development discussed above emphasises the symbiotic relationship between health and well-being and the interrelationships between the various factors that affect young children's health and well-being. The new discipline of *interpersonal neurobiology* is an example of consilience that embraces all branches of science to find a common, universal understanding of the mind and well-being (Siegel, 2012). In particular, evidence from the social, cognitive and affective neurosciences has led to an understanding that the brain is not simply an organ that enables us to think cognitively, but is a *biosocial* organ – in other words it requires external *social* interactions for growth *and* it needs to work closely with other *physiological* processes within the body (such as the stress response system), *and* it needs to pay particular heed to the role of *emotions* in order to optimise our health and well-being (Schore, 2001a; Porges, 2011; Immordino-Yang, 2011). This book therefore considers the interactions between different internal systems, such as the autonomic nervous system, alongside the external ecological system (Damasio, 1998). It also provides illustrations of interventions that work in an *integrated* manner with the brain, the body and the surrounding context to support young children's health and well-being – in other words practical strategies based on *psychoneurobiological* processes coupled with an *interpersonal environmental* approach (Schore, 2001a).

# The bioecological systems model of human relationships

The *interpersonal environmental* approach links closely to Bronfenbrenner's (2005) *bioecological systems theory*. This idea essentially acknowledges that many factors interplay to affect children's development and these manifest themselves in the early years largely through the personal encounters a child has with the environment and with other humans, along with the relationships that subsequently may develop. Bronfenbrenner envisaged a child's development in terms of the *interpersonal relationships* that the child encounters within systems of different (and increasingly complex) *environments* or layers of influence. These *layers of influence* have been named the microsystem, the mesosystem, the macrosystem, the exosystem and the chronosystem. According to Bronfenbrenner, it is the quality of the reciprocal relationships within these various systems that determines the nature of children's experiences and have a direct bearing on shaping human development. The microsystem is the layer (or layers) closest to the child and with which and with whom the child has direct contact, such as the immediate family, the neighbourhood and early years settings. The mesosystem is less tangible to envisage since it is conceived in terms of the connections or relationships between the various structures within the microsystems. The mesosystem comprises, for example, the interrelationship between child and parent. The early years' professional is another example of the reciprocal relationships encountered by the child within the growing microsystems.

The exosystem is easier to identify as this refers to the larger social system within which the child might not directly participate but it still has the potential to have an impact upon the child. For example, a parent's work place is part of the exosystem which might affect the amount of time a child spends in childcare. The exosystem thus may act as an indirect force shaping what relationships the child encounters in the microsystem. The macrosystem is less overt since it refers to cultural values, customs and laws that exist within or directly (and indirectly) dictate how the microsystems and exosystem operate. The macrosystem might affect the child through cultural norms or ideological blueprints that support a particular type of child-rearing practice or through legal frameworks such as a statutory early years curriculum. The macrosystem also incorporates broader issues such as socioeconomic status and ethnicity. The final layer is the chronosystem, which is another less tangible, but still influential, system and relates to events and transitions related to time that occur within the child's life. The chronosystem also entails wider sociohistorical circumstances such as changes in equal opportunities for women and the impact of these on young children's circumstances today via increased working prospects and consequent childcare issues.

The *bioecological systems* model focuses attention on an important theme in this book, namely that all the factors influencing a child are mediated by the child's *relationships* from conception to the start of school (and beyond). An important point to note, however, is that the child is viewed as an active participant within the relationships and environments, not a passive recipient. Indeed, Bronfenbrenner emphasised *mutual* interaction as integral to human development and noted how disruptions in one system had a knock-on effect on another. He considered that such influences were *bi-directional* which means that the relationships or structures within and between the different layers or environments are affected by and interact with each other. Moreover, Fleer (2005) warns against only envisaging contextual factors as operating as social influences *on* the child. She draws on Rogoff's (2003) views that children's learning and development is not only constituted by the external socio-cultural context but they also *contribute to* and *participate in* that context. This book certainly reflects this notion of the child as a contributing and active agent in the creation of the circumstances that promote their health and well-being.

## A relational model of health and well-being

The ecological systems model is now widely considered to be an effective model for supporting early childhood education and care, particularly for the most vulnerable (NSPCC, 2011). The NSPCC rightly identifies that 'at the heart of the model is the relationship between the primary caregivers and the child' (2011: 20). Similarly, the World Health Organisation (WHO, 2014) lists stable, responsive, and nurturing care-giving and safe, supportive, environments as the two main ingredients for determining health and well-being, (a third cornerstone is appropriate nutrition). Despite recognising children's active agency in their own development, this book focuses its attention on the *adult's role* in supporting young children's growth and progress and articulates how relationships are a powerful inoculation for children in relation to their health and well-being. Indeed, a recent research project on well-being in the early years identified that children viewed social relationships as central to their happiness (Manning-Morton, 2014). This book will reiterate throughout how relationships and the *quality* of these relationships with important adults are a major determinant of child health and well-being (Rees et al., 2013). It draws particular attention to the power of the relationship between practitioner and child, but acknowledges the critical role of familial relationships and the impact of this on children's immediate and ongoing health and well-being (Entwistle, 2013). The premise of this book therefore rests on the interactive process between a child's brain, body and surrounding relationships creating what Siegel (2012) refers to as the *triangle of well-being*.

## Structure of the book

The book begins by considering the role of the brain and body in health and well-being. Chapter 1 introduces the role and function of the brain in creating the adaptive behaviour necessary for health and well-being. It will set the scene for the complex interplay of environment and experience on brain function in relation to health and well-being, based on the biopsychosocial and psychoneurobiological models. Chapter 2 looks at the important features and processes that support health and well-being such as the connectome, plasticity, mirror neurones, pruning and tuning and vagal tone. Chapter 3 reviews the stress response system and highlights its significant role in affecting health and well-being. This is followed in Chapter 4 with a brief overview of the importance of nutrition and some key issues related to the nutritional dimensions of health and well-being.

The book then turns its attention to a focus on emotional health with Chapters 5 and 6 highlighting the significance of nurturing environments and experiences. Chapter 5 emphasises the importance of developing positive relationships between and within caregivers and young children by exploring attachment theory and the processes of interactional synchrony and attunement. Chapter 6 builds on the attachment relationship by highlighting the links to emotional development and, in particular, emotional self-regulation and the role of reflective functioning in supporting this. It also highlights the role of empathy and the development of emotional intelligence.

The next few chapters look more closely at the enabling environment practitioners can provide in their work with children. Chapter 7 initially focuses on the significance of active learning in promoting optimal health and well-being and highlights key aspects of physical development such as coordination, control and movement. The role of play is emphasised along with the importance of physical activity and interactive learning. Chapter 8 outlines the use of Emotion Coaching as a key strategy for helping to create an optimal, enabling environment and the promotion of nurturing relationships for emotional well-being and behaviour. It draws on a recent research project conducted by Rose and Gilbert (Rose et al., 2015). Chapter 9 turns its attention to more cognitive aspects of health and well-being by emphasising the importance of promoting self-efficacy and resilience in young children. The notion of Learning Power as a model for enhancing young children's health and well-being is explored.

The final chapters look at some of the broader issues that need to be taken into account when considering the factors that affect health and well-being, such as poverty, government policy, economics, inclusion and sustainability. Chapter 10 reflects on some of the challenges to resilience in health and well-being, such as poverty and trauma. The notion of early intervention is explored in Chapter 11 with examples of initiatives that have particular relevance to health and well-being. In doing so, the importance of integrating the inter-professional team around the child is emphasised alongside practitioner well-being. The final chapter provides an illustrative case study on the framework known as Five to Thrive. This framework draws together the key messages of the book and provides an effective model for early years practitioners to employ in their work with children and families in promoting health and well-being. The book concludes by identifying the need for a sustainable future in health and well-being. It highlights how practitioners can adopt an empowering approach for children to take ownership of their health and well-being, laying the foundations for sustainable health and well-being.

# Mindful Moments

Within each chapter there are some additional reflective activities or questions that will help you consider the implications of what you are reading for your own practice. We have called these *Mindful Moments* in order to draw attention to the importance of how adopting a *mindful* approach to your reading might enhance your understanding and awareness of the content. The *Mindful Moments* draw on some of the principles behind the practice of Mindfulness (Kabat-Zinn, 2006), such as pausing and contemplating on some of the things you have been reading, and thinking curiously and openly about them. Doing this should enable you to have greater awareness of your understanding and enable you to be more flexible and adaptable in how you translate this understanding into practice. They may lead you to take more considered action to create quality practice and in doing so potentially challenge habitual ways of working. Being mindful therefore operates in a similar way to *critical reflection* which entails questioning inherent values, beliefs and attitudes within personal and professional knowledge, including any practical wisdom and assumptions you might have about your practice (Rose and Rogers, 2012a). Also included in each chapter are chapter summaries, key points, suggestions for further reading and web links to useful resources.

# A cautionary note

It should be noted that, for the most part, this book does not address every aspect of health and well-being that might relate to young children. For example, we acknowledge the significance of pre-natal influences and the importance of nutrition on young children's development. However, we are unable to address fully the complexity of research on physical health and well-being within this book. Nor do we review the particular circumstances of children with additional needs or safeguarding issues related to health and well-being. Readers are also cautioned that it primarily adopts a Westernised perspective and therefore may not address cross-cultural dimensions.

Nonetheless, it does provide a concise overview of many central aspects of most young children's health and well-being, and emphasises the symbiotic relationship between health and well-being and the interrelationships between various factors that affect the majority of young children's health and well-being. In general, the book provides a solid foundation for all early years professionals in promoting young children's health and well-being, but perhaps the biggest message of all within this book is how the nature of a child's *positive relationships* with caregiving adults helps to pave the way for their optimal health and well-being (Shonkoff, 2010).

# CHAPTER 1

# BRAIN DEVELOPMENT – THE FOUNDATION FOR ADAPTIVE BEHAVIOUR

## Chapter Overview

This chapter introduces the reader to the wonders of our brains. It shows why all those who work with young children need to have an understanding of basic brain structure and function. It provides an insight into the neuroanatomy of the brain and the functional and maturational development pathways. In doing so, it will explore the physiological and psychological relationships between brain, body and mind and highlight the recursive and contingent connections between them. It also introduces the role of relationships and how interactions inform behaviours, which can inform early years practice and support the promotion of children's health and well-being.

## Why study the brain?

Have you ever wondered why some people seem to thrive in their lives while others seem to just survive? The survive or thrive outcomes were thought to be controlled by an individual's innate temperament and intelligence, or to develop from the opportunities of life experience. However, increasing collaborative research between neurosciences, behavioural sciences and education has questioned this traditional nature or nurture debate as too simplistic. It does not account for the complexity of human experience (Lewkowicz, 2011).

We now know that the brain is biologically programmed to support survival and to do this it follows a recognisable maturational development pattern. However, while our brains have similar basic structural components and common physiological processes, each brain is distinctive in its actual design and function. Neither genetics nor experiences can fully explain how each and every one has different behaviours and outcomes (Ridley, 2004). We live in a socially constructed world, and how we engage with information to sustain integration and achieve our goals influences the structure and function of our brains (Lewkowicz, 2011). Continual and recursive interactions with environmental, experiential and biological factors shape development trajectories, and it is in childhood that the brain is most receptive and malleable (Shonkoff and Garner, 2012).

The terms *mind* and *brain* are often used interchangeably. However, the mind should be seen as the *product* of the active processing of the flow of information in the brain. The brain filters, identifies and synthesises information to construct the mind, which then translates data into programmes of behaviour that are expressed through speech and actions (Greenfield, 2002). It is the cumulative interactions of the brain, mind and body that define our individuality. Therefore, as the mind is a metaphysical concept and it is challenging to objectively measure the relationship between it and the brain, we will examine both in subsequent discussions.

## Mindful Moment

From your own experience, what factors do you believe lead some people to thrive in life?

There is an increased scientific and educational consensus on how brains develop, function and are affected by environmental and relational experiences, and it is now considered important for those working with early years to have sufficient knowledge of the brain to support effective practice (Trevarthen, 2011a). To explore this idea further it is useful to use an analogy with something we are all familiar with and take as integral to our own lives and society: the car.

There are three levels of knowing cars. Most of us engage at level one: we know how to drive cars, know it has an engine that provides the power to move the car, and that cars are useful and integral to modern life. Some of us know cars at level two: these are the enthusiasts who know some of the basic components of an engine and understand what they need to work (for example, a car needs oil that needs changing periodically), know how to sustain performance (such as checking tyre pressure), know about common faults and can carry out basic repairs (such as changing a tyre). Then there are those at level three: the mechanics and engineers (the experts), who we turn to because of their specialised knowledge and professional skills to diagnose and treat any problem that we encounter. Most car users have some understanding of basic car maintenance but have to turn to a specialist to solve any problems that arise through wear and tear, misuse or poor maintenance. However, being an enthusiast enables you to independently sustain optimum performance and know when you need to seek specialist help.

The same can be said about caring for our brains: the brain is the engine that drives our lives. By being an enthusiast of the brain we can develop a more holistic understanding of child health and well-being. As an enthusiast, we can have an awareness of the basic structural anatomy and physiology of the brain, know how the brain and mind develop and how they connect *intramentally* (solitary thinking) and *intermentally* (communicating with others) (Rushton et al., 2010), and understand what influences performance and development (Zambo, 2008). This new knowledge about the brain will support professional confidence to create and sustain the environments and experiences that nurture children's learning (Immordino-Yang, 2011). Furthermore, given the correlations that appear to exist between health and well-being and economic outcomes, there is increased financial imperative for practitioners to recognise the functional relationships between the physical, social and psychological dimensions of human development (Trevarthen, 2011a). Practitioners need to feel competent in critically evaluating the credibility of research from many disciplines that purports to improve and sustain universal health and well-being, and particularly its relevance to effective practice. A clearer knowledge and understanding of the brain will help us to do this.

## The brain

A typical adult's brain has been described as 'big as a coconut, the shape of a walnut, the colour of uncooked liver and the consistency of firm jelly!' (Carter, 2010: 38) The brain is made up of *two cerebral hemispheres* on the right and left that are joined together by an information highway, known as the *corpus callosum*. The corpus callosum allows information to travel between the two hemispheres and it is believed that our *perceptions and memories* are products of the information that is *shared between* the left and right cerebral hemispheres (Cozolino, 2014). Brains are complex systems that have an innate self-organising capacity to balance the specialisation of areas with the connectivity of the whole in order to optimise brain efficiency and functional capacity (Siegel, 2012). We will divide the brain into *three* main areas, the *brain stem*, the *limbic system* and the *cortex* and briefly explore the structural features and functions of each of them in turn (see Figure 1.1 of the brain sliced vertically in half). For a more detailed explanation, see the suggested further reading list at the end of the chapter.

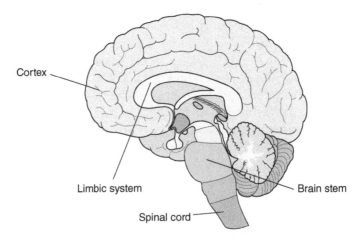

**Figure 1.1**   Areas of the brain

# Mapping the brain

Siegel (2012) has a very useful model which can help us visualise and better understand the situation of the different parts of the brain and how they are connected to one another. All you need is your arm and hand! Roll up your sleeve to reveal your model of the brain and central nervous system. Imagine that your arm is the spinal cord and that your hand is your brain. Now tuck your thumb across the palm of your hand and curl your fingers around it, making a fist, as shown in Figure 1.2. This is a now a simple 3-D representation of how the different regions of the brain are positioned and we can now explore how the different areas of the brain.

## Your arm and wrist: the spinal cord

All the messages from our muscles, internal organs and senses continuously travel up the *spinal cord* to the brain. In the brain, the information is

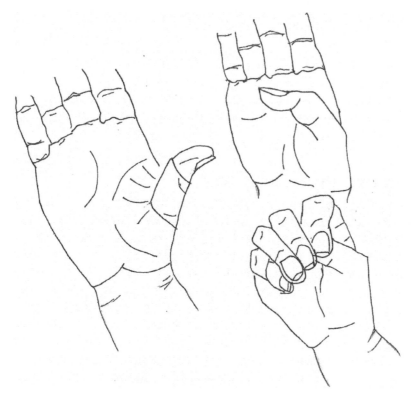

**Figure 1.2**  Hand model of the brain (Siegel, 2012)

(Illustrated by Christopher Walker)

decoded, prioritised and combined with previous knowledge, before being passed back down to inform a response in the muscles and organs. This to-ing and fro-ing of information happens consciously and unconsciously and is a process integral to our behaviours, whether we are awake or asleep, physically very active and engaged or sitting quietly and day-dreaming.

## Your hand: lower part of the palm: the brain stem

Your hand is joined onto the arm at the wrist and opens out into a palm. Imagine that the palm of your hand is the *brain stem*. The *brain stem* is where the nerves run up and down the spinal cord to join the brain (Figure 1.1). It is involved in unconscious (*autonomic*) functions, including the levels of alertness, breathing, heartbeat and blood pressure (all vital for living). The brain stem also facilitates the *fight–flee* mechanism – an essential survival response – which will be discussed in the next chapter.

## Your hand: lower part of the back of the hand: the cerebellum

The *cerebellum* (see Figure 1.4) is involved in integrating the sensory information passing into the brain, redirecting information to the different areas of the brain and controlling gross and fine motor movements as well as being involved in attentional levels and problem-solving (Badenoch, 2008).

## Your thumb: the limbic system

The *limbic system* is contained deep within the centre of the brain (your thumb is tucked away in the centre of your fist and surrounded by your hand), and so is referred to as being subcortical. It includes: the *amygdala*, the *hippocampus*, the *cingulate cortex*, the *hypothalamus* and the *thalamus* (see Figure 1.3). These specialised regions are not functionally mature at birth but are genetically primed to develop and connect as a result of relational experiences with primary caregivers (Badenoch, 2008). The limbic system, particularly the *amygdala*, is involved in prioritising behavioural responses to real or perceived threats for *survival*. It *continuously* receives, assesses and responds to external (environmental) and internal (organ status) information by comparing and

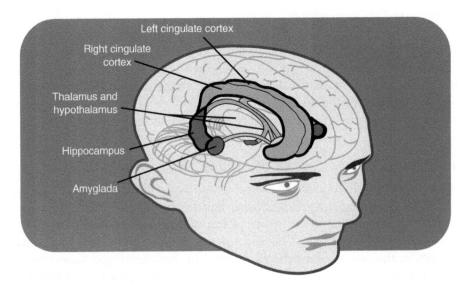

**Figure 1.3** The limbic system

combining streams of information coming into the brain with previous experiences that are stored as conscious (known) and unconscious (unaware) memories. It operates largely unconsciously and is significant to learning, motivation, memory, feelings and expressions of emotions, emotional memories and recognition of emotions in others (Carlson, 2007; Cozolino, 2014).

## Your hand: the cerebral cortex

The back of your hand, from above the wrist all the way to your finger-tips including the fingers themselves, represent the *cerebral cortex*. As you can see and feel, the cortex wraps closely around your thumb (the limbic system). The cortex has a convoluted (folded) surface and gives the brain its wrinkled walnut appearance. These convolutions increase the surface area (and so capacity) of the brain, while allowing it to be confined to a relatively small space (the skull). Two-thirds of the brain's surface is hidden in the convolutions and all *conscious and voluntary* behaviour including *thinking, talking, reasoning, reading, writing, understanding language, perceiving, empathy and planning* are carried out by the cerebral cortex (Carlson, 2007).

The cerebral cortex can be subdivided into *lobes* which have spe-cialised functions, although the function is not always exclusive to that particular location. These regions include (see Figure 1.4):

- *the occipital lobe* (back of the hand above the wrist): responsible for the processing of visual information, including shape and colour recognition;
- *the parietal lobe*: responsible for sensory processes, attention and language;
- *the temporal lobe*: responsible for the processing of auditory information and the integration of sensory information from other senses;
- *the frontal lobes, including the prefrontal lobes* (first joint after the knuckle to the finger tips): responsible for instigating and coordi-nating motor movements, for problem-solving, thinking, planning and organising, for the ability to attune to others and show empa-thy and compassion, to control impulsivity, to regulate the body and to calm fears, and for emotional and personality traits (Keenan and Evans, 2009). Because the frontal lobes and the limbic system work so closely together to inform behaviour, we will discuss them in more detail below.

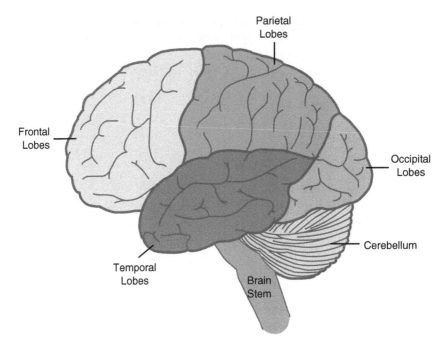

**Figure 1.4** Lobes of the cortex

## Your first joint after the knuckle to the finger tips: frontal lobes

This part of the finger represents the frontal and prefrontal lobes of the cerebral cortex. Notice how your fingers (frontal and prefrontal lobes) are in direct contact with your thumb (limbic system) and palm (brain stem): the limbic system is tightly held by the frontal and prefrontal lobes. The prefrontal and frontal lobes are the most evolved part of the brain and control thinking, perceiving, planning and understanding language – all informing conscious actions and behaviours.

Because there are more connections between the frontal lobes and the limbic system than in any other area of the brain, basic emotional responses, which are generated unconsciously in the limbic system, influence frontal lobe activity. We often hear phrases such as 'she flipped her lid' or 'he's lost his marbles' when referring to behaviour in response to emotionally charged situations. If you open up and flip all your fingers up to expose your thumb, this demonstrates what happens in the brain when we feel under threat – the connections are lost.

# What happens when we feel threatened?

If the limbic system detects a significant threat, it bombards the frontal lobes with warning messages to prepare the body for action and support survival. The body responds by re-directing energy to the limbic system and restricting energy flow to the cortex, making it more difficult to think straight and behave rationally. Early years practitioners can often witness toddler tantrums, which reflect the flipping the lid brain response. Toddler tantrums are a *normal* part of development and reflect the immaturity of connections between the limbic system and the developing frontal lobes. For toddlers, threats can be real or perceived, such as obstacles to achieving goals or a thwarted desire (Goleman, 1995). As the frontal lobes mature and connections are strengthened, the child learns from experience and can adopt more reasonable behaviours to express their needs. However, if the connections to the frontal lobes are under-developed, which can be seen in children who have not experienced nurturing relationships, the knowledge and skills needed to assess options for action may be compromised and the resulting behaviours may be unhelpful (Shonkoff et al., 2012).

Although the limbic system's primary focus is on survival, when the frontal lobes perceive the environment is safe, they can override the stress response and enable pro-social behaviour to occur (behaviour that encourages positive social interactions). This is a *bi-directional relationship*, whereby the limbic system provides emotional labels that inform appropriate responses from the frontal lobes and the frontal lobes signal to the limbic system to adjust the stress response. Future chapters will explore ways in which practitioners can support the connections between the limbic system and the frontal lobes, for example Emotion Coaching (see Chapter 5) can help young children learn to regulate their emotional responses and moderate behaviour.

## Mindful Moment

Try to think of a situation when emotions were running high for you – how did you feel? Were you in control of your actions and were your actions the most effective way to resolve the problem?

Check out the hyperlink to Daniel Siegel talking about flipping the lid at: https://www.youtube.com/watch?v=G0T_2NNoC68.

# How is information processed in the brain?

A *neuron* is the basic type of cell found in the brain (see Figure 1.5) and connects with other neurons to create *neuronal networks* which collectively are known as the *connectome* (Seung, 2012). Neuronal networks are communication highways that allow information to travel all around the brain. At birth, a child's brain contains roughly the same number of neurons as an adult, which is between 89 and100 billion (Carlson, 2007). Each one of these billions of neurons has the capacity to connect to other neurons thousands of times. However, young children's neurons are *immature in function* and have *restricted network connectivity*. As the brain matures neuronal networks integrate, bringing the brain parts together to function as a whole. Typically, the increasingly dense and complex connectome allows for more efficient engagement with greater volumes of information, enabling the child to participate in more complex experiences, environments and relationships. Neurons cannot store energy so require a constant supply of nutrients and oxygen. The brain's activities use 20 per cent of our total energy intake (Carlson, 2007), so if we want our brains to function well they need to be properly fed!

# How do neurons work?

Figure 1.5 shows a typical neuron. Information in the brain is passed as *electrochemical pulses* through each neuron. Notice the tree like branches, known as *dendrites*, which receive information from other

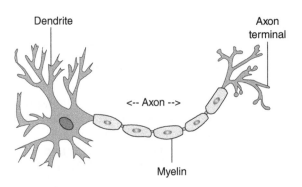

**Figure 1.5**  A typical neuron

neurons. The message then passes along the *axon* into the axon terminal. Here there is a *synapse*, a junction between the axon terminal and the dendrite of the next neuron. The information is passed across the synapse by the secretion of *neurotransmitters*. The *receiving* dendrite then takes the information and passes it down its axon into its terminal, and so it continues like a chain reaction. Every neuron has *many* dendrites and axon terminals. Therefore one neuron can be connected to multiple neuronal networks, all transmitting information to and from different areas of the brain. However, only if the electrochemical pulses are frequent or strong enough will the information pass through the neuron and onto the next neuron in the network. So it is the *strength* and *frequency* of the electrochemical pulses that affect the *efficiency* of the neuronal networks and the *speed* at which information can be processed. Strong and frequent pulses build robust connections that allow information to travel quickly.

## Typical brain development

A child's brain and connectome grows dramatically during the first few years of life and by the time a child is two years old, the brain has increased to such an extent it is three-quarters of the size and weight it will reach as an adult (Keenan and Evans, 2009). Brain maturation progresses from the back of the brain to the front, with the *brain stem* (linked to bodily regulation), the *thalamus* (for sensation) and the *cerebellum* (for movement) showing most activity from birth (Carter, 2010). This provides the baby with the coordination needed to engage with the environment and to communicate survival needs. The *frontal lobes*, the areas concerned with rational decision-making, judgement and planning, are the last to mature and are not fully developed until a child reaches their twenties (Shonkoff and Philips, 2000).

Brain function is affected by the level of physiological maturation (time), genetic make-up (genes) and interactions with the environment (experience) but hinges upon relationships with others (people). A child's development thus reflects cultural and social experiences as well as physiological maturation. As a social organ the brain is shaped by living experiences; there is a synergy in that children learn to live and so live to learn. Therefore, early life experiences are particularly important because this is when the brain is growing rapidly and the foundations of the mind are being laid. These ideas will be revisited in the following chapters when we discuss the physiological mechanisms that the brain uses to learn.

## Mindful Moment

If our brains were simple enough for us to understand them, we'd be so simple that we couldn't (Cohen and Stewart, 1995: 8).

The unusual names given to areas of the brain and how the brain functions and communicates with the body are complex and can be confusing, especially if this information is new to you.

Thinking back to the beginning of the chapter and the analogy of there being different levels of understanding and engagement in cars, explain how you would like to see yourself in relation to the brain: as a user, an enthusiast or an expert?

## Key Points

- Environmental and experiential factors contribute *positively or negatively* to the building and maintenance of the brain.
- Foundational brain-based skills, such as thoughts, actions, dreams, creativity and resilience, support children's learning and promote health and well-being.
- These skills reflect the complex recursive relationships between the brain, the environment, life experiences, relationships and our genes.
- Providing nurturing experiences and relationships are considered foundational to building brains that have the infrastructure to effectively engage and adapt throughout the lifespan.
- Having a better understanding of the basic functions of the brain and typical patterns of development is critical to creating and sustaining an early years environment that allows all children to flourish.

# Useful Further Reading and Websites

- Carter, R. (2010) *Mapping the Mind.* London: Phoenix Press. This provides useful summaries about the brain with some interesting case studies.

- Siegel, D. (2012) *The Developing Mind: How Relationships and the Brain Interact to Shape Who We Are*. New York: Guilford Press. This is a very readable and canonical text for any enthusiast of the brain.
- Visit the website: http://www.brainfacts.org/ for lots of information, articles and great visual aids. Download the free 96-page book at: http://www.brainfacts.org/about-neuroscience/brain-facts-book/.

# CHAPTER 2

# BRAIN PROCESSES IN HEALTH AND WELL-BEING

## Chapter Overview

In this chapter we will explore how the brain functions and the physiological processes that contribute to a child's health and well-being. First, we will develop an understanding of the brain's neuronal networks or *connectome*, its ability to develop competency and capacity, and how behaviours become automated. Secondly, we will explore *plasticity* and how the brain interacts and responds to changing environments. Thirdly, we will discuss how the neuronal networks are constantly under review and are *pruned and tuned* by experience, environment and genetic programming. As we will discover, this does not always result in improving health and well-being! Finally, we will examine how specialised neurons, *mirror neurons*, thought to be involved in helping us to better understand others' intentions and emotions, provide evidence of the necessity for good role modelling and nurturing social interactions to support young children's learning.

## Why is it important to know how the brain functions?

Awareness of the brain's typical development and the factors that shape the connectome to modify memory, creativity, empathy and emotional control, empowers the practitioner to create healthier and nurturing settings. Knowing how children learn to make sense of their environments, experiences and relationships, and how memories and immediate stimuli are combined to inform behaviours, further validates the adult's facilitative role in children's learning (Rushton, 2011). Although neuroscience offers a fascinating insight into the working of the brain, practitioners should adopt a critical approach to the translation of research into educational settings (Rose and Abi-Rached, 2013; Howard-Jones, 2014a). This will help to guard against misinterpretation of brain science or inappropriate applications in practice. By adopting the persona of a car enthusiast (see Chapter 1) and having a sound understanding of the brain and how it functions, we can ensure practice fosters healthy development to support health and well-being.

# The connectome

As noted in Chapter 1, *neurons* are specialised cells that allow the brain to process information. They form dense networks and collectively these are referred to as the *connectome*. The connectome carries all the information used to inform decisions and actions. Messages picked up by dendrites pass down the axon and leave the neuron via the synapses. These synapses can be either be *excitatory* or *inhibitory* and they can either *speed up* or *slow down* messages. This is because intelligent behaviour involves the ability to make appropriate responses but also to recognise when it might be necessary to inhibit a response, such as controlling an impulse to react aggressively when feeling threatened (Geake, 2009).

We are born with far more neurons that we will ever need, but a baby's neurons are not well connected and do not function as efficiently as an adult's. As we age neurons can develop more connections and so increase the complexity of the connectome and join up the different areas of the brain. Neuronal efficiency is further improved through *myelination*, which occurs through maturation and by repeated neuronal stimulation (Carlson, 2007). In myelination, the *axons of the neurons* become coated in an insulating layer known as the *myelin sheath* that improves the conductivity between neurons by up to three thousand times, so dramatically increasing the efficiency of the connectome (Siegel, 2012).

The connectome is also established, strengthened and advanced in *capacity* and *function* by *repeated stimulation* of the neurons, highlighting the importance of repetition for learning. By establishing specific patterns of neuronal networks children are increasingly able to represent the world mentally (Schaffer, 2004). Frequent use not only encourages the growth of dendrites and axon terminals, allowing more connections, but also improves the *functional efficiency* of the networks.

Therefore, as children get older, they are able to understand more, engage in more complex experiences and contribute to more sophisticated communications. In this way, they build *cognitive frameworks* or *mental representations* of the world. By repeated stimulation, certain neuronal networks become the preferred routes and are more sensitive to receiving, sending and storing information. With maturity, the brain develops a greater capacity to store and use information (mental representations) that drives our thinking and actions.

One way to visualise how the connectome develops and functions is to think about road maps. Road maps provide a pictorial overview of a country, show the transport network system and help you to navigate. Imagine your brain as a country, made up of different regions, and each of the regions is populated with towns. The connectome is the road transport system which connects the towns and regions of the country, your brain. It is the *quality* and *quantity* of this transport system that will directly influence your ability to get to visit the towns, regions and the country as a whole. If you looked at a map and saw that the various towns you need to visit are some distance from one another and in different regions, you would then look for the roads that connect up the towns. You will inevitably search for the quickest routes which will let you visit all the towns. If you see that connections between the towns are few and the roads are all small, you know that the journey will be slow and difficult. However, the more often you do the journey, the more familiar the roads become and you will complete the journey in less time and effort. If dual carriageways were built on the most popular routes, the journey time between towns would be reduced, allowing you to visit these towns more easily and often. What if a motorway was then built between towns joining up with the dual carriageway? For convenience and speed, this would then become the most popular route and these towns would thrive while the towns connected by slower routes become less sustainable and might die.

This analogy is particularly helpful when thinking about the structure and function of children's connectomes. We know that children's neuronal networks are immature – made up of narrow roads that are not well connected – so information takes more time to travel around the network. In areas that are not well connected, information can end up unprocessed, misunderstood and even lost. For a child to have the best opportunity to be able to utilise all their brain to support their learning, they need to develop and maintain neuronal networks that are made up of major information motorways that are well integrated and interconnected. Early years practitioners can play an important role in helping to build these motorways.

> ## Mindful Moment
>
> When thinking about the brain we advocate imagining a landscape that is covered in a huge communication network.
>
> Make a list of what you think are the advantages of having a communication network that is extensive and well-connected. What might be the disadvantages of not having access to a reliable, easily accessible communication network?

# Brain plasticity

Although children are born as innate communicators and competent learners (Trevarthen, 2011b), their brains are physiologically immature and unable to function independently. Initially, everything needs to be learnt and they are dependent on their caregivers for all their physical, psychological, social and emotional needs. The brain continually tries to make sense of the world by engaging with it and this engagement alters the structure and connectivity of neurons and neuronal networks. Every time a neuron *fires*, it reinforces, extends and strengthens the neuronal synaptic connections, creating a more effective network as we saw earlier. This is known as *neuroplasticity* or *brain plasticity*.

Neuronal networks undergo a constant honing and toning of function through repeated experiences that strengthen pathways and develop capabilities. In 1949, Donald Hebb (Geake, 2009: 48) noted that neurons that *fire together, wire together* and, as we saw in the previous section, it is the *frequency* and *strength* of stimulation that increases the quality of connectivity. So the more often a neuron is stimulated, the more likely it is to connect to other neurons and build stronger, faster connections allowing more information to be processed. If stimulation is repeated often enough, the neurons can become so sensitive that an *automated* chain reaction of a whole network of neurons can be activated with very little stimulation. However, we must also remember the *recursive* aspect to the creation and maintenance of our neuronal networks. Our behaviour and actions reflect the functional efficiency of our connectome, but the experiences that result from our behaviours and actions also feed back, further shaping the neuronal networks. Thus the brain shapes *and* is shaped *by* actions and behaviours (Shonkoff and Garner, 2012). This ability to use experiences to create new neural pathways that increase and improve connectivity in the brain is most prolific in childhood, but the good news is that brain plasticity continues throughout life, albeit at a much slower rate.

Another key point to note about neuroplasticity is that adaptions in the connectome are driven by an innate survival instinct. When children lack adequate nurturing opportunities or feel unsafe, this can have an accumulative negative effect on the structural and functional capacity of the connectome (Child Welfare Information Gateway, 2009; Shonkoff and Garner, 2012). Their developing neuronal networks focus on supporting survival in the hostile environment in which they live. However, although these adaptive and behavioural responses are protective and help survival, they are often less effective in supporting  pro-social behaviours or cognitive learning in other environments, such as the early years setting. These processes are discussed further in Chapter 11.

## Tuning and pruning

Earlier we pointed out that children are born with *more neurons than they will ever need*, although the majority are immature and poorly connected. Genetic, environmental and experiential factors sculpt the neuronal linkages and so the scope of the connectome, particularly in childhood. Therefore, because neurons and neuronal networks thrive through *frequent, varied and repeated use* brain development is *activity-dependent*. It is the activity in and between the neurons that shapes the sensory, motor, emotional and cognitive neuronal networks. Nurturing, multi-sensory experiences and repetition helps to *tune* neurons to work together to become more efficient and effective in their connectivity (Cozolino, 2014). This process is known as *synaptogenesis* (Carlson, 2007).

Maintaining the growth of neuronal networks requires large amounts of energy and puts a high demand on the body's limited energy supply, so neurons that are not used become redundant and are destroyed by *pruning* or *apoptosis* (Carlson, 2007). This is essential to healthy brain development as pruning away inefficient neurons prevents the brain becoming overfilled with redundant networks. This allows the remaining networks to work more quickly and efficiently and strengthens the well-used connections. However, pruning is a process that occurs to any neuronal network that is not regularly stimulated, whatever its function or potential purpose. As Seung (2012: 95) notes 'the connectome is where nature meets nurture', so children who have experienced trauma or neglect will have connectomes that have been tuned and pruned for survival. Brain scans of such children confirm poorly connected brain regions, sparser neuronal networks and patchy brain activity (Shonkoff and Garner, 2012). This could, in part, explain why these children have difficulty in memorising information, adapting to new environments and embracing new experiences (Nelson et al., 2011). In cases of extreme neglect it is believed that certain areas of the brain do not develop at all and, although brain plasticity can later go some way to ameliorate early deprivation, sometimes these children never gain optimum brain capacity (Behen et al., 2008).

As practitioners, it seems we should not underestimate the power of positive engagement and experience on brain development. In particular, nurturing early years' experiences *helps to build brains* that have the infrastructure and capacity to support and sustain effective learning. Brain plasticity offers a strong physiological explanation for pedagogical practice that supports the promotion of learning environments that are consistently nurturing, multi-sensory and experiential. As discussed earlier, we also know that children learn from others and through life experiences, therefore it is vital that we recognise the importance of effective role modelling and better understand its influence on children's health and well-being. The next section highlights some specialised neurones that are thought to offer further explanation as to how we influence and are influenced by others, and how our brains use these neurones to learn from and learn to be with others.

## Mirror neurones

*Mirror neurones* are specialised networks found mainly in the frontal and parietal lobes that are believed to help to encode information about the external world and goal-directed behaviours in ourselves and others (Rizzolatti and Sinigaglia, 2010). They are also likely to be involved in our ability to learn manual skills, gestural communication, spoken language, group stability and empathy (Cozolino, 2014). Mirror neurons help us to distinguish between differing actions as well as infer the intention of others. So, for example, they help us to differentiate between an arm raised for help, waving in welcome or held up in anger. It is believed that mirror neurones become activated when we perform an intentional action *or* observe others' actions or expressions, such as facial expressions, bodily stance, gestures, tone, pitch and volume of voice. By triggering our mirror neuronal networks we have a visceral-emotional experience (bodily sensation) of the observation (Siegel, 2012). Think about how you feel when you see a friend crying, a child reaching up to an adult for a hug or an elderly man struggling to carry a heavy bag? Most of us can imagine the sadness of that friend, the pressing need of the child and the old man's discomfort without having to actually experience it. It is the activation of our mirror neuronal networks in response to others' actions and emotions that let us indirectly experience their emotions. This ability to understand the intent behind others' actions elicits a more *empathetic* response allowing communication in more meaningful ways. Repeated activation of these mirror neurones establishes *implicit* memories (not consciously having to be recalled) about the actions and intentions of others (Badenoch, 2008). These experiences, whether positive or negative, are used to create an evolving understanding of what the world is about and how best to respond to situations.

Rushton et al. (2010) believe that the *actions*, *reactions* and *interactions* that occur between the child and an adult are the most important factors in determining the learning outcomes and development of a child. If the adult or the child is unable to predict another's intention, or finds it difficult to interpret, it can lead to poor levels of communication or miscommunication. Therefore early relationships need to provide many empathetic and nurturing experiences to help establish an effective and  pro-social mirror neurone system that can support sensitive engagement and understanding between the child and others. Although children are born as competent and effective communicators, adults do have to learn to *attune* to a child in order to be able to interpret and respond appropriately. Children actively engage and co-construct in this relationship and in doing so they learn to expect specific responses from their main carers (Balbernie, 2007; Trevarthen, 2011b). The child develops its own communication repertoire from these early relationships and *imitation* is one of the tools humans use to communicate. From birth, babies can copy facial gestures, which are central to interpersonal attunement and group coordination (Cozolino, 2012). Siegel (2012: 311) believes that 'attunement of emotional states is essential for the [child's] developing brain to acquire the capacity to organize itself more autonomously', and by watching and copying others a child learns how to engage in relationships and the environment. Therefore childhood is a significant time when children can develop and practise the skills needed to understand and engage in an adult world. These ideas are revisited throughout the book, particularly Chapters 5 and 6.

## Mindful Moment

A model which effectively summarises the key qualities and functions of the brain, is the 4 C's:

- *Connections*. The connections between neurons and neuronal networks need to be established, extensive and efficient to utilise the whole of the brain's capacity.
- *Contributions*. Children live and learn from significant others about their roles, rights and responsibilities. These contributions help to shape their developing brains.
- *Co-construction*. The functional efficiency of brains reflects co-construction between genes, environments, experiences and relationships. It is an evolving, ongoing, lifelong relationship.
- *Creativity*. To promote brain health and well-being children need to be personally engaged in environments, experiences and relationships that are nurturing, multi-sensory, rewarding, motivating, interesting and fun.

Think about your own brain and how it has been shaped by experiences. Can you think about a time when you learnt a new skill – were mirror neurons involved? What helped you to become proficient? What helped to support your learning?

## Key Points

- Neuronal networks (the connectome) are the brain's communication system, connecting the different areas of the brain. To support learning we need brains that have strong, fast and reliable connections that can allow all areas of the brain to be involved.
- Neuroplasticity is the brain's innate capacity to learn from experiences and environments. Neuronal networks are shaped and strengthened by repeated exposure to experience and environments, whether these are nurturing or hostile.
- Mirror neurons are thought to be involved in learning to understand the actions and intentions of others and in the development

*(Continued)*

*(Continued)*

of empathetic behaviours. They are activated through the child's relationships with others and their environment.

- Building the connectome is a very energy-demanding activity. If neurons are not activated frequently, they are pruned and connectivity in that area of the brain can be compromised.

## Useful Further Reading and Websites

- The website of the Centre of the Developing Child based at Harvard University has an excellent resources section including videos, lectures and research papers at: http://developingchild.harvard.edu/.
- Young Minds, a leading UK charity committed to improving the emotional well-being and mental health of children and young people, has a useful section devoted to the neuroscience of well-being at: http://www.youngminds.org.uk/training_services/young_minds_in_schools/wellbeing/neuroscience.
- Rose, N. and Abi-Rached, J. (2013) *Neuro: The New Brain Sciences and the Management of the Mind*. Princeton, NJ and Oxford: Princeton University Press. This book discusses the emergence of educational neuroscience and includes a critical discussion.
- Law Nolte, D. and Harris, R. (1998) *Children Learn What They Live*. New York: Workman Publishing. This book explores the influences on childhood learning and the poem on which the book is based is available at: http://www.nytimes.com/2005/11/20/arts/20nolte.html.

# CHAPTER 3

# THE STRESS RESPONSE SYSTEM IN SUPPORTING HEALTH AND WELL-BEING

## Chapter Overview

We will explore the recursive relationships between the brain, body, emotions and behaviour, recognising that behaviours can be constructive or destructive and have immediate and accumulative effects on health and well-being. Experiencing some degree of stress is a necessary part of a normal life. With supportive relationships, good social interactions, and nurturing environments, life experiences help to develop coping and resilience skills. However, extreme or persistent stress, or relationship and environmental privation, can compromise physical health and mental well-being, especially when experienced in early childhood.

## Regulation of bodily functions

To function effectively, the brain, mind and body need a consistent, internal environment. *Homeostasis* is the physiological function that regulates the body's functions. This mechanism works through an *autonomic* or subconscious nervous system that optimises function. It ensures that all systems work together, but can also respond independently to additional demands and return back to normal as these demands subside. It both influences and is influenced by the strains of normal living and is involved in the activation of the stress response system.

Both *real* and *perceived* threats trigger a stress response through the autonomic nervous system. The secretion of hormones, which are chemicals made in the body that affect the functioning of bodily organs, allow our bodies to quickly adapt our behaviour to promote the best chances for survival, whether that be to fight, to flee or to freeze. Once the threat is over, all systems quickly return to normal functioning levels so that energy is not wasted. Homeostatic function can become compromised if the stress response system is frequently activated and is not able to recuperate. In terms of evolution, *the autonomic stress* response is a primitive mechanism to be alert and prepared for danger. It ensures that energy supplies are mobilised and that the body responds quickly and efficiently to the trials and tribulations of hunting and gathering food. However, although we no longer need to hunt and our environment is not populated with danger-ous wildlife, the autonomic stress response persists and is now triggered by *different* kinds of stressors (Goleman, 1995). These modern-day threats include social, economic and relational dangers such as bullying, poverty and loneliness. Although these stressors are more socially constructed, they activate the same autonomic physical responses in the body: *to fight, to flee or to freeze*. These responses may be physically impossible or socially inap-propriate and, consequentially, can be transformed into feelings of anxiety, agitation, hyper-vigilance and depression (Schore, 1994). These feelings are difficult to ignore, and the resulting repetitive and sustained activation of the stress response leads to compromised health and well-being rather than survival (Porges, 2011).

### Mindful Moment

Think about your own life and the modern-day stresses you encounter on a daily basis. Which stresses seem manageable and which ones may overwhelm you? How do the stresses make you feel?

## Emotions and memories

Everyone has emotions that have a primacy to support survival through adaptive behaviour. Some, such as distress, fear, surprise, joy, disgust and anger are innate and universal: we are all born with them. However, others, such as envy, guilt, pride and shame, appear from toddlerhood and are dependent on the values and norms of a child's environment and relationships (Cozolino, 2014). Emotions play a significant and integral role in learning, in that they help to focus attention to determine the significance of the environment and motivate behaviours (Davidson and Begley, 2012).

Information is received consciously and unconsciously through our senses, and needs to be processed by the brain before action can be taken. An *emotional label* is given to all stimuli, as this helps the brain to categorise the information, identify potential threats and so prioritise responses. This happens *automatically*, mainly in the limbic region of the brain (Woltering and Lewis, 2009). Any stimulus is also referenced against *implicit memories*, which are memories of early experiences and relationships that are stored unconsciously in the brain. As long as the emotional label does not activate a significant stress response, the information is sent for conscious, rational processing, which includes referencing with explicit memories in the cortex and prefrontal cortex. *Explicit memories* are memories that are conscious and intentional recollections of previous experiences and information. Memories are stored as series of connecting neuronal networks and combined with the current information to inform behavioural responses (Seung, 2012). We will look again at the way in which implicit memories are stored in the brain through our relational experiences in Chapters 5 and 6.

## What controls our response to stressors/threats?

The *autonomic* nervous system has two components: the *sympathetic* and the *parasympathetic* systems. The autonomic sympathetic nervous system supports all actions related to getting going (mobilisation), which includes our ability to respond to threats by activating survival behaviours. This is known as the *defence stress response* and is driven by the fight or flight mechanisms. The autonomic parasympathetic nervous system supports actions to promote *im*mobilisation. This is carried out largely by the *vagus system* which has direct contact with all the major organs in the body and acts as a control or brake on the stress response system. It is also associated with digestion, relaxation, growth and recuperation of the body (Panksepp, 1998).

Traditional explanations have suggested that behaviour is driven by the presence or absence of threats, and controlled by the paired interaction of the autonomic nervous systems (Carlson, 2007). When the environment is deemed safe, the parasympathetic nervous system suppresses the sympathetic nervous system inhibiting defensive responses and allowing social interaction. When there is a threat, the parasympathetic nervous system control is reduced allowing the body to be prepared to fight or flee. However, is this explanation too simplistic to fully explain the variety and complexity of behaviours seen in society? For example, in response to extreme threats, some individuals go into behavioural shutdown or freeze rather than fighting or fleeing. These behaviours do not support mobilisation so it is difficult to know how they promote survival and why, in spite of adverse life experiences and relationships, we still continue to seek social interactions.

Porges' (2011) Polyvagal Theory recognises the role of social intelligence to offer a further explanation of the complexities of human behaviour and stress. Social intelligence is considered an 'inherent, intrinsic, psychobiological capacity that integrates perceptual information from many modalities to serve motive states' and is reliant upon and leads to cultural learning (Trevarthen and Aitken, 2001: 4). Porges (2011) suggests that, because of the necessity to engage in an increasingly complex and socially constructed world, our brains have evolved and adapted to become more intricate and sophisticated in function. We still retain ancient circuits for survival; however, our autonomic nervous system has evolved and is composed of *three* rather than *two* (sympathetic and parasympathetic) *phylogenetically* (*evolutionary*) organised subsystems. This creates a *hierarchical* social communication response system and the *social engagement subsystem* is the *most recent* and preferred mode for social communication. It *dominates* the other subsystems which come into play if the social engagement subsystem fails. By seeing the defence stress response system as a part of a hierarchy of social communication responses rather than independent, both the commonality and the diversity of children's behavioural responses to potential and actual stressors can be better understood.

# The Polyvagal Theory

## Subsystem 1: Social engagement system

To communicate, we prefer to use the Social Engagement System. This uniquely mammalian, myelinated, vagal motor circuit *supports positive social interactions* by inhibiting sympathetic nervous system activities which might otherwise mobilise us to act defensively or overreact. It is associated with the active processes of attention, motion, emotion and communication, all necessary for effective social interaction (Porges, 2011).

We continuously – and largely unconsciously – scan our environments to anticipate potential and actual risks. This process, known as *neuroception*, happens both internally (bodily pain, fever or physical illness) and externally (dangerous person or situation) (Porges, 2011). Neuroception allows us to monitor and update our safety status, ensuring that our behaviours and body's physiological states are matched and appropriate. Part of this process involves detecting and evaluating the body and face movements and vocalisations of others. These are *cues* processed by the brain and contribute to our overall perception of a person's safety and trustworthiness, guiding us as to whether it is safe to approach or not. If neuroception identifies that a person or situation is safe, then the myelinated vagus nerve actively inhibits defence behaviours of fight or flight or freeze to engage in pro-social behaviour. The myelinated vagal circuit also alters the muscles in the inner ear, so we are able to be more tuned into speech and less focused on lower frequency sounds that are synonymous with threat and predators (Porges, 2011).

To develop social bonds, not only does the stress response mechanism need to be inhibited, but we need to also be able to reduce social distance and physically engage. Yet we know that babies take several years to gain voluntary control over motor behaviour, so how can they develop social bonds? Social bonding is possible because, at birth, the neuronal networks that control face and head muscles are sufficiently myelinated, allowing babies to actively engage with a caregiver. Babies use vocalising, grimacing, gazing, smiling and sucking to engage in co-constructing social bonds. Through interactions with caregivers they learn to create facial expressions, gesture with their head, put intonation in their voice, direct gazes and distinguish human voices from background sounds. When we feel safe and secure, a hormone called *oxytocin* is released which helps to establish and cement social bonds. Repeated experience of positive emotions increases our sense of social belonging and boosts parasympathetic health. Neuronal networks are established and are strengthened through repetition of experience which support further social interaction and engagement. This in turn encourages and supports further positive, social connections and promotes physical health, creating an 'upward spiral dynamic' in health and well-being (Kok et al., 2013: 1128).

As this myelinated vagal motor circuit originates in the same area of the brain that controls the muscles of the face and head, facial expression and voice intonation can also be coordinated to convey *cues to others* that we are not a threat. Therefore the myelinated vagal motor circuit is both expressive and receptive, and this is why hearing a calm voice instils calmness. Anything in the environment that is perceived as threatening – and for a baby it can be something as simple as a change in a familiar face's muscle tone leading to a loss of expression – causes a shift in neuroception from safe to dangerous (Tronick, 1998). The myelinated vagal circuit is then turned off, disrupting any opportunity for spontaneous, interactive and reciprocal social engagement.

In typical development a child's neuroception accurately detects risk. However, the frequency and quality of social engagement and care and opportunities to experience nurturing environments can lead to either adaptive or *maladaptive* defensive behaviours. If a child has an inability to inhibit their defence systems in a safe environment, or an inability to activate their defence mechanism in a dangerous environment, there can be immediate and accumulative detrimental consequences to their health and well-being (Allen, 2011).

## Mindful Moment

Based on the well-known work of Tronick (1998), the still face experiment shows what happens to a young child when her mother does not engage. It is a powerful visual example of the social engagement system and shows how quickly the stress response system becomes activated. Watch the YouTube clip at the weblink below and think about the baby's reactions to the mother's still face: https://www.youtube.com/watch?v=apzXGEbZht0.

## Subsystem 2: Mobilisation and the stress response system

Stimuli that are high, persistent or unfamiliar or emotionally labelled as *fear, anger* or *disgust* signal a threat to our basic need for self-preservation and safety. The *limbic system*, believing the threat may compromise survival, will *override* the social engagement system and automatically initiate the stress response system.

The stress response system is activated through the sympathetic branch of the autonomic nervous system. It results in feelings of anxiety, panic and agitation and further raises awareness of the threat. Hormones (natural signalling body chemicals) such as *adrenaline* and *cortisol* are released to stimulate the physical changes needed in the body to enable rapid response. (See Part 1 of Table 3.1 to view the effects on the body from the activation of the stress response system (Carlson, 2007; Schaffer, 2004)).

**Table 3.1**   Maintaining homeostasis: our react, response and return mechanism

| Part 1: The sympathetic nervous system<br>*How the stress response system affects our body and brain* | Part 2: Parasympathetic nervous system<br>*Returning bodies back to normal function* |
| --- | --- |
| ➢ Increases sensitivity and awareness to potential threat | ✓ Reduces awareness to threat |
| ➢ Increases startle response | ✓ Reduces startle response |
| ➢ Increases sensitivity to environment | ✓ Reduces awareness to environment |
| ➢ Secretion of stress hormones | ✓ Stops stress hormone release |
| ➢ Increases heartbeat | ✓ Reduces heart rate |
| ➢ Lungs take in more oxygen | ✓ Returns breathing rate to normal |
| ➢ Increases blood pressure | ✓ Reduces blood pressure |
| ➢ Increases blood flow to muscles, limbs and brain | ✓ Slows blood flow |
| ➢ Increases blood sugar levels to increase energy supply | ✓ Reduces blood sugar levels |
| ➢ Breakdown of proteins and mobilisation of fats for instant energy supplies | ✓ Slows breakdown of protein and mobilisation of fats |
| ➢ Brain activity changes to more instinctive (guided by the limbic system) | ✓ Connections to frontal lobes are re-established so as to improve access to rational, cognitive thinking |
| ➢ Immune response decrease | ✓ Immune response readjusted |
| *Unnecessary bodily functions are minimised to maximise energy supply for survival functions* | *Bodily systems are restored to normal baseline function* |

With the mobilisation of energy sources and temporary suppression of all non-essential bodily functions, the body is prepared to respond by either fighting for survival or fleeing from the threat. However, this response to stressors and maintenance demands a lot from the body and is not designed to be activated frequently, as it cannot be maintained for long periods of time without it becoming detrimental to health and well-being. Therefore, as soon as a threat is deemed to have passed, the parasympathetic system is activated and all bodily systems return to normal functioning levels. It is only when the stress response is inactive that we can relax and use energy supplies to support growth and recuperation of the body. (See Part 2 of Table 3.1 for the specific effects of the parasympathetic nervous system on the body that helps to calm us down).

## Subsystem 3: The unmyelinated vagal motor circuit

This is the most ancient and primitive of the three systems and refers back to humans' reptilian ancestry. It is only activated when both the social engagement system and the sympathetic nervous system (defence fight/flight mechanism) are no longer available or effective. This response acted as a reptilian defence mechanism by immobilising and dramatically reducing heart rate and breathing. The immobility meant that the predator would either no longer be able to track its prey, or that animals apparently dead would be considered to be potentially disease-ridden and therefore not eaten (Maclean, 1990).

However, for humans, immobilisation can be dangerous. Immobilisation as a result of extreme fear is driven by the *unmyelinated* vagus nerve circuit. When children are unable to protect themselves by either using social engagement or fight/flight strategies, they can experience behavioural shutdown. This results in being unable to move (from a source of fear) or *dissociating* from their environment and carers. If a child feels impotent they will be unable to communicate their needs or engage in active learning, but their responses could be misinterpreted as intentional or disruptive, or may suggest collusion. However, what they are evidencing is the most extreme survival response to perceived dangers (Cozolino, 2014).

Although we are all driven by survival needs it should be remembered that children's brains are developing and so are immature in structure and function. Therefore, it is the ongoing combination of the maturational process and brain functions, such as mirror neurones and neuroplasticity, that shape their neuronal networks and the speed at which information can be processed. Children's behaviour, including the activation of the stress response, reflects the frequency, intensity and quality of their experiences, relationships and environments. Brains that have been flooded with stress hormones, or have had to frequently activate the stress response, will develop efficient neuronal circuitry that allows *hyper-vigilance* of their environment and of others, with *lower thresholds* to activate the stress response system (Sunderland, 2007).

## Case Study

### Early experiences and the stress response system

Jay is five years old and lives with her mother, her five siblings and a stepdad. She is her mother's fourth child and her older brothers are at secondary school. They are often in trouble for truancy and poor behaviour. Her four-year-old brother has special needs as he has recently been diagnosed as having restricted vision and partial deafness. Jay has moved house five times since her mother left her father, but none of their homes have been in a good state of repair or in child-friendly neighbourhoods. Because her mother works long hours, Jay has to rely on her brothers for support and care. She has no daily routine and eats whenever and whatever she can. Her brothers argue a lot, play a lot of violent computer games and often settle disputes with physical violence. Jay tries to keep away from her stepdad who works night shifts and has a short temper and argues with her mother.

Jay is a small, undemanding child in Reception class, who finds it difficult to express her needs and becomes distressed if she is the centre of attention. She has difficulty in settling to play, often drifting from one activity to another, especially if the play is to be shared with others. She is quick to use physical aggression to solve disputes with her peers and is verbally abusive to staff when they try to intervene.

*To effectively promote and sustain health and well-being for children, we must be aware of and sensitive to the dynamics that influence their particular worlds. From what you now know about the brain, how do you think Jay's experiences have affected her stress response system and how she views relationships and how people behave?*

## Vagal tone

*Vagal tone* is the ability to assess and *respond* to threats and then *return* the body and brain to a normal functioning state (Diamond et al., 2011). It is shaped by a combination of genetic, environmental and experiential influences, and develops throughout childhood (Gunnar and Donzella, 2002).

Children with *better vagal tone* have more responsive vagal circuitry, and they are able to respond more quickly, process information faster and concentrate better. As a result, their responses to stimuli are deemed more appropriate and effective, and they show an ability to quickly return to a normal resting state. This minimises additional demands allowing the body and mind to focus on the restoration of homeostasis and growth, including learning. Better vagal tone is linked to better emotional balance, clearer thinking, improved attention, a more efficient immune system and greater resilience. Children with *poorer vagal tone* have lower levels of responsiveness so they respond to and process information less quickly and are less able to concentrate for longer periods of time. Their responses to stimuli may be less appropriate or ineffective and they have difficulty, when aroused, returning to a normal resting state (Gottman et al., 1997).

For very young children, vagal tone is initially activated via access to *safe and secure relationships and nurturing environments*. Usually these are provided by the child's main carers whose contingent responses *attune* to a child's distress and responds to their needs (Trevarthen, 2011b). By showing compassion and offering physical and psychological comfort, the child's response system is soothed physiologically and psychologically they return to a calmer state.

Therefore, it is evident that young children are reliant on *significant others* to satisfy their needs. However, as they grow older, and through frequent opportunities to share and learn, offering repeated occasions to recognise, practise and adapt behavioural responses in nurturing environments, children learn to *self-soothe* and *self-regulate*. As a result of brain plasticity both detrimental and nurturing experiences shape vagal tone. It is therefore important to be aware of what can be or become a stressor for children, so as to optimise opportunities for the development of good vagal tone. We explore these ideas further in Chapters 5, 6 and 8.

## Mindful Moment

Earlier in this chapter we asked you to think about stressors in your life. Have a look at Figure 3.1. It represents vagal tone by showing someone trying to recover balance after a stressful experience, and return the body, mind and brain to homeostasis. What helps you to restore balance?

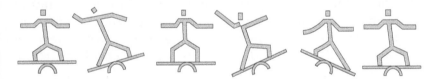

**Figure 3.1**   Vagal tone: maintaining a balance

(Illustrated by Christopher Walker)

# Stressors in children's lives

The extent to which a stressful event has a lasting adverse effect is determined by an individual's response to stress. This is *mediated* by genetic predisposition, which includes temperament, so some children are born with better vagal tone. However, many other factors affect our capacity to moderate stress, including the availability of *supportive relationships* and the *duration, intensity and context* of the stressful experience (Seligman and Harrison, 2012).

Through role models and experience we can learn to influence our stress response. If emotional arousal is low and neuroception suggests that the environment or person is not a major threat, then the frontal lobes, which are well connected to the amygdala, override activation of the stress response by accessing memory and using rationality to reduce the perception of threat and arousal. An example of this could be when you have to go to the dentist. You may feel scared and not want to go, but you tell yourself that you know teeth need regular checks, that the dentist has no intention to hurt and any treatment will be covered mostly by painkillers. You can effectively *override* your (conscious or unconscious) stress response system which is perceiving the dentist as a threat and remain calmer. Adult brains have a greater capacity to do this because with maturity and experience comes the ability to process, combine and utilise information more effectively.

There are three types of stress: *positive, tolerable* and *toxic* (NSCDC, 2014).

## Positive stress

This is the kind of stress that everyone needs to develop skills in order to cope and is essential for healthy development. A young child's stress response may be activated when they are hungry, cold or feeling insecure. In a nurturing environment, the physiological effects are *buffered* by supportive, reliable adults who help to activate the child's vagal circuitry, supporting the return of all systems to baseline norms. Experiences of *short-lived* stress which is made *manageable* through the consistent and empathetic care of adults helps to develop their vagal tone. It is because of brain plasticity and mirror neurones that these experiences establish the brain architecture and neuronal networks to effectively deal with stress. As the child matures, the repeated experiences become memories and support the development of adaptive responses that restore the stress response system to normal. In time, the child can learn to *self-regulate* without a supporting adult and develop a resilient, healthy stress response system. We will reconsider positive stress in later chapters when we explore how positive stress can promote learning.

## Tolerable stress

This is when stressors are more serious or prolonged and the body's stress response system is activated to a *greater* degree. An example of this may be experiencing a frightening injury or the loss of a loved one. However, again, if this stress is time limited and buffered by supportive relationships and environments, then the child can recover. Support from nurturing adults helps the child to *adapt* and *move on*, and so not permanently compromise their stress response.

## Toxic stress

This occurs when a child's stress response system is *continually* activated by stressors that are strong, frequent, traumatic or prolonged with *inadequate* supportive, relationships or adverse environments. Physical and emotional abuse, chronic neglect, caregiver mental illness and economic hardship are stressors that can, if unchecked, lead to a chronic activation of the child's stress response system (Gunnar and Quevedo, 2007).

As noted earlier, maintaining a stress response demands large amounts of energy and so all non-essential bodily functions are reduced (as per Table 3.1). Multiple exposure to toxic stress can lower the threshold of the child's stress response, leading to frequent and longer activation. Prolonged activation of the stress response can result in disruption to the development of a child's brain architecture. Toxic stress causes connections in the neuronal networks to be reduced or lost while also weakening organs and the immune system (NSCDC, 2014). This increases the risk of stress-related diseases and cognitive impairment which can have ongoing effects in later life (Shonkoff et al., 2009).

If a child has experienced a lot of stress in their life, or has caregivers who are unresponsive, unpredictable or unable to support their needs, then their brain adapts by prioritising the development of skills to *survive* in the hostile environment. Chronic abuse can lead to an increase of neural connections in the regions of the brain related to fear, anxiety and impulse response. This happens at the expense of establishing strong neural connections in regions dedicated to reasoning, planning and behavioural control. These adaptions affect cognitive abilities and pro-social skills. Balbernie (2001) summarises that early detrimental experiences can lead to:

- learning difficulties
- language delay
- lack of empathy
- hyperactivity/ disruptive behaviours
- distractibility
- hypervigilance
- poor impulse control
- lack of compassion.

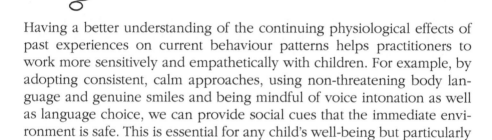

## Mindful Moment

Take a look at the resource link below from the Center on the Developing Child at Harvard University. There are a number of excellent articles and videos about the effects of stress on a child's developing brain.

- http://developingchild.harvard.edu/key_concepts/toxic_stress_response/

Having a better understanding of the continuing physiological effects of past experiences on current behaviour patterns helps practitioners to work more sensitively and empathetically with children. For example, by adopting consistent, calm approaches, using non-threatening body language and genuine smiles and being mindful of voice intonation as well as language choice, we can provide social cues that the immediate environment is safe. This is essential for any child's well-being but particularly for those who have experienced extreme levels of stress.

## Key Points

- Vagal tone reflects the child's ability to respond to stimulus and return bodily functions to a normal, balanced state.
- Genetics, temperament, relational experiences and environments have a profound influence on the development of a child's vagal tone and their ability to engage in pro-social behaviours and active learning.
- If a child feels unsafe or insecure in their relationships or environment their stress response system is activated. Physiological changes occur in their brain and body to support actions for survival, compromising their ability to focus on learning or access rational thoughts.
- The stress response system demands a lot of energy and is designed to only be short-acting, returning the body to normal function levels as soon as possible.
- Prolonged or extreme stress can have a devastating effect on bodily systems including the immune system and the developing brain architecture.
- Stimulating, nurturing environments and empathetic relationships are believed to support the development of neuronal networks that support self-regulation.

## Useful Further Reading and Websites

- Sunderland, M. (2006) *The Science of Parenting*. London: Dorling Kindersley. This book provides valuable insights into how we can promote emotional well-being in young children, drawing on the neuroscience discussed in this and the previous chapters.
- Conzolino, L. (2014) *The Neuroscience of Human Relationships, Attachment and the Developing Brain*. New York: W. W. Norton. This is a very readable text that discusses in detail the issues introduced in this book.
- The Anna Freud Centre is a clinical, educational and research institution specialising in the psychological treatment of children. It is dedicated to children's emotional well-being and is a national charity: http://www.annafreud.org/.

# CHAPTER 4

# NUTRITION IN HEALTH AND WELL-BEING

---

## Chapter Overview

This chapter provides an introductory overview of how nutrition affects physical and cognitive development. It considers relevant issues such as obesity, relationships with food and the importance of developing sensible eating habits during the early years. The chapter ends with suggestions on how food can be employed as a medium for learning in early years settings.

---

## Nutrition and its role in health and well-being

It is self-evident that children require a healthy diet to satisfy their biological needs and enable them to develop and grow to their full potential. Food is broken down into its component parts in our body and then used to build our body's tissues and structures and to ensure the smooth running of body processes. Evidence shows that poor nutrition affects our cognitive functioning and academic potential (Albon and Mukherji, 2008). Therefore, knowledge of the nutrients and their role and function within the body is essential. Maslow's hierarchy of needs emphasises food as a basic physiological component to be satisfied before an individual can progress (Maslow, 1954). The social and environmental aspects of nutrition, such as cultural attitudes to food and eating, the availability of foods and access to quality healthcare are the subject of much controversy and susceptible to trends and popular media representations. Furthermore our relationship with food and our eating behaviours incorporate a psychological dimension. Conner and Armitage (2002) believe that our underlying *beliefs* about food and whether or not foods are *perceived* as healthy or unhealthy will influence our choice of food and eating behaviour. Thus healthy eating can mean different things to different people.

Essentially, there are five key nutrients: *protein, carbohydrates, fats and oils (lipids), vitamins* and *minerals.* In addition, we need *water* and *dietary fibre.* For health and well-being we need a *balanced* diet containing foods from each of these groups in the *right proportions* according to the body's needs. Individual needs differ according to age, gender, state of health and physical activity. Children need regular meals to get the energy and right nutrients to support growth and well-being (BDA, 2014). Ideas about what constitutes the right proportions of nutrients have changed over time, contributing to the confusion and sometimes misinformation surrounding ideas about nutrition and health. The current NHS (2014b) Eat Well Plate recommends higher intakes of complex carbohydrates (starchy foods) and fruit and vegetables, smaller proportions of protein and dairy foods, reduced amounts of high fat and sugar foods and low salt intakes.

Consuming insufficient food to meet the body's energy requirements results in *undernutrition* whereas *malnutrition* arises from deficiencies of specific foods or inappropriate quantities of food (Shetty, 2003). For example, someone could have ample food but consume excess fat; or eat appropriately for their energy requirements but be deficient in specific vitamins. If, during childhood, essential nutrients are missing or depleted this can impede growth and cause deficiency diseases. For example, anaemia can result from inadequate iron intake and rickets from vitamin D deficiency. In a *well-balanced* diet our food intake should supply all the nutrients required and we should not need food supplements. However, supplements may be medically prescribed for specific illnesses and conditions, and at certain times in the life cycle, for example pregnancy and old age.

Table 4.1 provides a summary of the main nutrient groups which affect young children's health and well-being. However, this is a generic review which does not address specific cultural preferences and individual dietary needs (including safeguarding issues such as allergies and metabolic conditions, including diabetes). For a more detailed account of nutritional needs and effects on health and well-being, practitioners are encouraged to consult the websites suggested at the end of this chapter.

**Table 4.1** Table of nutrients

| Nutrient | Types | Sources | Function |
|---|---|---|---|
| Protein | *High biological value* – contains all 8 essential amino acids | HBV – meat, fish, eggs, cheese, milk | Growth and repair; secondary source of energy |
| | *Low biological value* – essential amino acids limited or missing | LBV – nuts, pulses, cereals | |
| Carbohydrates | Sugars – simple | Sugar, honey, cereals, sauces, jams, cakes, sweets | Energy Note: Excess carbohydrate converts to body fat |
| | Starches – complex | Potatoes, cereals: rice, wheat, pasta, flour, bread | |
| Fats | Saturated fats | Butter, cheese, lard, suet, fat in meat, cream | Long-term energy; transports fat-soluble vitamins; protects organs in body; component of cells and hormones; dense source of calories for EY children |
| | Unsaturated fats/oils | Vegetable oils, oily fish, nuts | |
| Vitamins | A | Carrots, liver, green vegetables, tomatoes, dairy foods | Healthy immune system; vision in dim light; healthy skin and mucous membranes |
| | B group | Cereals, bacon, bread, yeast, green vegetables, bananas | Neurological development; nervous and digestive systems |
| | C | Fruits and vegetables, particularly citrus fruits | Healthy skin and gums; prevents scurvy |
| | D | Sunlight acting on the skin; dairy foods, oily fish | Healthy bones and teeth; prevents rickets |
| Minerals | Iron | Red meats, cereals, green vegetables, egg yolk | Haemoglobin in blood to transport oxygen round body; prevents anaemia |
| | Calcium | Milk, butter, cheese, cereals, green vegetables | Strong bones and teeth |
| Water | | Milk, fruit juices, fruit, vegetables, drinking water | In every cell; regulates body processes; in blood, saliva and digestive juices |
| Dietary fibre | | Fruit and vegetables, bran, wholemeal bread, grains, seeds and nuts | Aids digestion; prevents constipation; protects against bowel cancer |

High intakes of saturated fats, found in dairy produce and meat, have been linked to coronary heart disease (CHD), strokes, narrowing of the arteries, high blood pressure and raised cholesterol levels in later life, but Lean (2006) notes that other factors can confound the results and it is difficult to isolate fat as the sole causal factor. Unsaturated fats found in vegetable oils such as olive, rapeseed and sunflower oils, avocados, nuts and seeds, have been found to lower cholesterol levels in the blood (Hark and Deen, 2005).

Our bodies cannot store vitamin C so a daily intake is required. Neonates, infants and young children might not get sufficient vitamin C from their diet alone (Hasselhölt et al., 2012), particularly if they are selective fussy eaters, commonly seen between 18 months and five years (BDA, 2013). Since low intakes of vitamins are common in babies and young children, the UK government recommends that children aged six months to four years should take vitamin A, C and D supplements, unless they drink 500 ml of infant formula a day, which has vitamins added (BDA, 2014).

Iron is critical, for the development of the brain and healthy neuro-development, particularly in the first two years of life. Deficiency at this age can impair future cognitive and behavioural and physical development (Domellöf and Szymlek-Gay, 2012). However, caution must be exercised as there are adverse effects of having excess iron when deficiency has not been identified.

Calcium and phosphorus are needed in conjunction with vitamin D for healthy bones and teeth. The soft and growing bones of the neonate, through a process of calcification, develop into hard structures that are capable of supporting the growing body.

Water is needed in every cell in the body. Dehydration negatively affects the cognition and concentration levels of children (Edmonds, 2012; Leibermann, 2007). Over 50 per cent of UK children have inadequate hydration (Gandy, 2012) so access to water for young children is important.

## Mindful Moment

Compile a list of the food and drink you consumed yesterday. Were there foods from each nutrient group and did you have a *balanced* diet? Are there changes you could make?

# Child obesity and health and well-being

The UK is ranked as one of the most obese nations in Europe. According to National Child Measurement Programme statistics (PHE, 2014), 9.5 per cent of children attending reception class (4–5 years) during 2013–14 were obese and 13.1 per cent were overweight. Heart disease, high blood pressure, orthopaedic problems of the feet, leg and back, Type 2 diabetes, hyperlipidaemia, high cholesterol and an increased risk of some cancers and liver disease are just some of the physiological consequences of obesity and its impact on current and future health and well-being is serious (Dovey, 2010). Obesity is associated with overeating but this is not the sole cause. The biopsychosocial model considers how heredity (genetics) and socio-environmental and psychological factors play a part. For example, Straub discusses links between genetics and obesity but concludes that heredity cannot be responsible alone and that 'regular activity and a healthy diet can limit genetic tendencies toward obesity' (Straub, 2014: 292). Ogden (2012), drawing upon the research of Hill and Peters (1998), refers to the *obesogenic environment*, where children have reduced opportunities for activity and exercise because of increased car travel, less walking, spending long periods in front of the television and computers and parents fearful of children playing outside. Such factors, coupled with diets high in fat and an increased consumption of carbohydrates, particularly sugars such as high fructose corn syrup (HFCS), have contributed to the rise of obesity (Tucker, 2011). Larkin (2013) describes the *vicious cycle of childhood obesity*, whereby lack of exercise and poor diet make children susceptible to weight gain. This lowers their self-esteem and they avoid exercise. Their weight increases causing mobility problems; exercising becomes difficult and they develop health problems such as Type 2 diabetes, asthma and strained joints and muscles. This means they then cannot exercise and so put on more weight.

Obesity problems in young children can be linked to parents who inaccurately assess their children's weight, overestimate activity levels, underestimate the amount of fat and sugar that is consumed, provide portions that are too large for children and make no connection between poor diet, low exercise and potential long-term health risks (Larkin, 2013). Even in households where there is an awareness of healthy eating practices, food may be used as a bargaining tool to elicit good behaviour (Dwyer et al., 2008; Ogden 2012). It follows that if high fat, high sugar snacks are presented as treats, this creates an association of pleasure with such foods and if they are not normally allowed such foods, this sensation can be heightened.

There are also social and emotional effects as obese children can become socially isolated and targets for bullying, which damages self-esteem and has a detrimental impact on their emotional health and well-being (Conner and Armitage, 2002). Mansfield and Doutre's research (2011) identified that children viewed obesity negatively and they believed that obese children made poor choices and had poor self-control. However, there was also empathy to try to protect obese children from discrimination.

## Relationships with food

Albon and Mukherji (2008) consider the socio-cultural significance of food and mealtimes and how they are intricately linked to our sense of personal and cultural identity. The UK Office for National Statistics (ONS, 2014) highlighted research showing how family mealtimes can strengthen family bonds and the child's sense of belonging. The benefits of families eating meals together are associated with better eating habits and decreased risk of obesity. Moreover, family mealtimes are thought to be an important factor for happiness in family life: if mealtimes are happy and relaxed, they will promote health and well-being. Conversely, if there are tensions, this will affect children's emotional well-being and could lead to negative associations with food.

Children learn their eating behaviour through social learning, that is from observing and modelling their behaviour on others around them (Ogden, 2012). They can develop strong likes and dislikes based on their experiences and observations (Siegler et al., 2014). Children are usually good at self-regulating their food intake, but parents can become overly concerned about what they are eating and how much (Siegler et al., 2014). This may result, for example, in overeating, as children are encouraged to clear the food on their plates. This can set a precedent for future eating habits, such as overeating (McCaffrey and Livingstone 2009). Underdown (2007) refers to the *cycle of anxiety* whereby parental anxiety can be sensed by the child making mealtimes a difficult experience for both, leading to insufficient consumption by the child and increased anxiety. *Emotional eating* has also been posited as a reason for unhealthy eating patterns leading to weight gain with individuals confusing the signals and responding to stress in the same way as they would if they were hungry (Conner and Armitage, 2002). The following case study provides a positive example of food being used to achieve a regulating effect with young children.

## Case Study

### Food and self-regulation

James, a five year old, was referred by his school to a sensory integration therapist to improve his physical coordination and behaviour.

Food was used to support James's well-being. It can have a regulating effect by helping to calm children and meet physiological needs as well as emotional nurturing. Crunchy foods can be successful for calming anxiety and chewy foods can be used to dissipate anger, such as chewy, buttery toast or bagels.

James completed a programme with his occupational therapist and parents designed to help children to self-regulate their emotional states and behaviour through sensory activities such as eating. Food (crunchy carrot sticks and cereal) was used as a regulating snack to support James in school for circle time; as a result he managed to sit through this, whereas before he sat at the back on his own as he could not settle easily.

Linda, Occupational Therapist (http://www.therapyspacebristol.co.uk/)

# Learning through food

The importance of instilling healthy eating behaviour in the early years cannot be underestimated. Initially parents and caregivers have sole responsibility for the child's food-related experiences, but early years settings can provide opportunities to encourage children to extend their knowledge and experience of food and eating behaviours. Furthermore, activities involving food provide opportunities for learning an extensive range of skills as suggested below.

## Mindful Moment

### Learning through food

Consider how food can be used as a medium for learning in the early years setting utilising food-based activities to empower young children to develop a wide range of knowledge and skills related to healthy eating. Table 4.2 should help you to identify key areas.

*(Continued)*

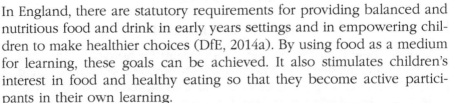

*(Continued)*

**Table 4.2**   Learning through food

| Area of knowledge/skill | Teaching and learning |
| --- | --- |
| Practical | Developing gross and fine motor skills and hand-to-eye coordination – handling, chopping, cutting, peeling. Planting seeds to grow their own food – digging, tending, picking, harvesting, preparing, cooking (and eating!) the produce. |
| Nutritional | Thinking about why we need food and what food is good for us. |
| Scientific | Learning about the nature of food and how heating and mixing changes it. Learning about the body and what foods we need. |
| Geographical | Increasing knowledge of where food comes from and where it grows, including other regions and countries. |
| Maths | Weighing and measuring ingredients, counting the produce, looking at costs of food. |
| Hygiene | Remembering the importance of washing hands, tying hair back and wiping surfaces clean before food preparation. |
| Multisensory learning | Experiencing new foods, smells, tastes and textures. |
| Food production | Growing food in the setting's garden and thinking about how we cook and make the things we eat. |
| Language and cognition | Discussing how to carry out the task, following instructions, interactive role modelling. |

In England, there are statutory requirements for providing balanced and nutritious food and drink in early years settings and in empowering children to make healthier choices (DfE, 2014a). By using food as a medium for learning, these goals can be achieved. It also stimulates children's interest in food and healthy eating so that they become active participants in their own learning.

To promote healthier lifestyles there needs to be multi-level intervention at different levels – child, family, policy, cultural – to prevent unhealthy habits from becoming the norm in childhood, particularly for those in areas of high socio-economic disadvantage (Mansfield and Doutre, 2011).

## Key Points

- Perceptions of healthy eating depend upon pervading attitudes and values.
- A balanced diet consists of the key nutrients in the correct proportions.
- Obesity levels are rising and various biopsychosocial factors compound this situation.
- Early years settings can encourage healthy eating through food-based activities.

# Useful Further Reading and Websites

- This is a UK government-sponsored website explaining how the government supports children's health and well-being at: https://www.gov.uk/government/policies/giving-all-children-a-healthy-start-in-life.
- Healthy Start is a UK government scheme to improve the health of low-income pregnant women and families on benefits and tax credits. This site provides information at: http://www.healthystart.nhs.uk/.
- The British Dietetic Association (BDA) provides information on healthy diets with a dedicated section on children and babies at: https://www.bda.uk.com/foodfacts/home (for an alternative information source see NHS Choices).
- This site provides useful guidance for feeding under fives in a childcare setting at: http://www.publichealth.hscni.net/publications/nutrition-matters-early-years-guidance-feeding-under-fives-childcare-setting.
- The European Food Information Council provides a comprehensive overview of nutrients and their functions at: https://www.eufic.org.

# CHAPTER 5

# ATTACHMENTS AND EARLY RELATIONSHIPS

## Chapter Overview

Chapters 5 and 6 turn their attention to the emotional dimensions of health and well-being and the crucial role played by early nurturing environments and experiences in laying the foundation for emotional health. Traditionally, child development policy and practice has focused on physical health and cognitive development. However, in recent years increasing attention has been paid to the importance of *emotional* well-being in forming the basis for healthy physical and cognitive development. In this chapter, we will emphasise the significance of early relationships through an exploration of early *attachments* and the *attunement* process in developing positive relationships between caregivers and young children. The key principles of attachment theory are outlined and the attunement process is explored by reviewing some dimensions of *interactional synchrony*. It will highlight how attachment relationships help to develop significant neural connections within the brain, forming a basis for effective stress regulation and creating what is known as the *Internal Working Model*. In essence, the chapter demonstrates the centrality of early relational experiences in establishing health and well-being. A further chapter will build on this to consider how attachment relationships help to create emotional self-regulation.

## Attachment – the foundations of emotional health

This chapter begins by outlining one of the fundamental tenets of early child development – *attachment theory*. The evidence base for this seminal theory is now considered to be a gold standard by world-leading organisations such as the United Nations (NICE, 2012). Attachment theory has been defined as 'a long-enduring, emotionally meaningful tie to a particular individual' (Schaffer, 1996: 127). It is essentially a relational process whereby a strong affectional bond develops between one person and another. The theory has primarily focused on the infant–caregiver attachment relationship, which has been shown to have long-lasting consequences on health and well-being.

Attachment theory emerged in the previous century from the work of Bowlby (1969) (a British psychoanalyst and child psychiatrist) and Ainsworth (1979) (an American developmental psychologist). Bowlby's initial work in supporting young people with behavioural difficulties led him to believe that the nature of the relationship between a mother and baby had a profound impact on the child socially, psychologically and biologically. Bowlby drew on a range of disciplines to develop his theory including evolutionary biology and developmental psychoanalytical concepts which highlighted an infant's innate disposition to seek closeness and protection from a caregiver, driven by the need to survive and cope with environmental stresses. This process led to particular adaptive systems within the brain and body which managed the infant's capacity to cope with the stress of living. As we saw in earlier chapters, because young babies' neural circuits are immature, they are entirely reliant upon caregivers around them to regulate their stress and help them to satisfy their deep need to feel safe and secure. The caregiver's responses to the infant's stress, whether this is driven by purely physiological needs (such as hunger) to psychological drives (such as the need to feel loved), directly affects how the infant then learns to cope with the stress of life as they begin to mature and take on a greater capacity to meet their own needs more independently. Essentially attachment theory proposes that a caregiver who consistently, sensitively and appropriately responds to a distressed child will promote what was termed a *secure* attachment (Ainsworth and Bowlby, 1991). Alternatively, caregivers who are unresponsive, insensitive or inconsistent in responding to their child's distress signals promote an *insecure* (or *anxious*) attachment. Robust, long-term studies have overwhelmingly shown that securely attached children generally have higher self-esteem, better emotional self-regulation and more resilience when adults than children with insecure attachment histories (Sroufe and Siegel, 2011).

# Modern attachment theory: the neuroscience of attachment

Attachment theory has undergone various revisions as more research has unearthed other dimensions to the process of attachment. For example, Bowlby's original assertion that attachment ought to take place between mother and child has been broadened to include any caregiver, and it is recognised that multiple attachments can occur as long as they are sufficiently consistent as well as responsive (Schaffer and Emerson, 1964; Sroufe, 1995). Recently, technological advances have enabled us to access more easily the internal mechanisms of the brain and neuroscientific research has endorsed the original attachment theory. Two leading academics in America (Allan Schore and Dan Siegel) have paved the way in forging links between traditional attachment theory and recent discoveries about the brain.

Allan Schore is known as the American Bowlby. His extensive work on *affect regulation* has highlighted the psychoneurobiological mechanisms through which attachment relationships are formed (Schore, 2001a), that is how the early emotionally laden attachment communications that occur between infant and caregiver help to wire the maturing brain (Schore, 2014). The term affect regulation relates to the *emotional* functioning of brain development, both the physical and psychological aspects (Howe, 2011). Schore (1994, 2001a, 2001b) draws on his own and others' brain-based research to show how neural connections develop out of the limbic and autonomic nervous system into the upper cortex. You may recall that these processes were discussed in more detail in the first three chapters. Schore's work has shown how these connections follow a particular patterning and are essentially a management or control system (as Bowlby initially described it), which enables the child to learn to cope with and manage the stress of living. The particular neural connections that are forged are entirely dependent on human interactions for optimal development and lay foundations for the entire life cycle.

These developments rely on the *reciprocal* exchange of visual, auditory and tactile sensory information between infant and caregiver and formulate a psychobiological core in helping to develop attachment security (Schore, 2001a). Other neuroscientific research has also shown how, for example, facial expressions, posture, tone of voice, actions and movements all play a role in stimulating the infant's nervous system. For example, research by Feldman et al. (2011) has revealed how an infant and mother's physiological states (such as their heartbeat) literally adapt and adjust to each other in a synchronous manner. (Some of these ideas are explored further below in the section on interactional synchrony.) These processes demonstrate how social and emotional development evolves in direct correlation with *physiological* and *biological* processes, which hinge upon the capacity to regulate stress and the generation and maintenance of a state of emotional security. A child's emerging social, psychological and biological capacities in turn hinge upon the relationship with the caregiver. As Schore writes:

The infant forms a secure attachment bond of emotional communication with the mother, and this early socioemotional learning is then internalized in the form of an enduring capacity to regulate and thereby generate and maintain states of emotional security. (2001a: 203)

Dan Siegel, a clinical psychiatrist, is another key theorist in modern attachment theory who has undertaken research which affirms the enormous significance of attachment relationships in promoting health and well-being. In this book, his hand model of the brain has been drawn upon to outline the key neurological processes involved in the development of the brain and the stress response system. He has also developed a useful framework for understanding the key principles behind the attachment process and how it can be promoted (Siegel and Bryson, 2011). This framework consists of the 4 S's of attachment, namely – *Seen, Safe, Soothed* and *Secure* (see the Mindful Moment below).

## Mindful Moment

### The 4 S's of attachment

- *Seen* – This is more than just being seen visually – it is about perception and letting a child know that they are perceived deeply and empathically, that we see inside the child's mind and what lies beneath their behaviour. Siegel calls this *mindsight*.
- *Safe* – This is about helping children have a sense of safety by avoiding actions and responses that might frighten or hurt them.
- *Soothed* – This is about making sure that we help to regulate children when they are experiencing difficult emotions and stressful situations, enabling them to calm down.
- *Secure* – Being seen, feeling safe and being soothed helps to establish a sense of feeling secure so that children develop an internalised sense of self and personal well-being, which in turn empowers them to explore and learn about the world.

(Adapted from Siegel and Bryson, 2011)

Think about your own work context or work experience – in what ways does the practice help to fulfil the 4 S's of attachment?

Siegel's framework builds upon two key notions within Bowlby's (1988) original attachment theory, namely the concepts of *secure base* and *safe haven*. The secure base/safe haven is provided by the attachment figure, usually the primary caregiver, who not only provides the infant with food, warmth and protection but becomes the figure that provides close contact and proximity, and calms and soothes them. As the infant grows and gains more mobility, the safe haven becomes a secure base – a source of confidence and security to start exploring the world around them. The child continues to view the attachment figure as a safe haven – someone they can retreat to in times of stress and uncertainty. When they have recovered and feel safe, they can venture from what is now perceived as their secure base and return to their explorations. This process has implications for early years practice as attachment theory demonstrates that a child needs an empathic and supportive attachment and relationship with their practitioner to optimise their brain development.

Research has also shown that adults other than the immediate caregiver can act as potential *secondary* attachment figures for children (Sroufe and Siegel, 2011; Commodari, 2013). Although this might not be a fully fledged attachment bond, nonetheless early years practitioners can be attachment figures for young children and develop an *attachment-like* relationship (Bergin and Bergin, 2009). In England, each setting is obligated by law to assign a Key Person to each child in order to help the child become familiar with the setting, offer a settled relationship for the child and build a relationship with parents – in other words provide a secondary attachment figure for the child. In addition, they need to ensure that every child's learning and care is tailored to meet their individual needs (DfE, 2014a). The need for a Key Person is of particular significance given that the *attachment system* (the innate drive to feel seen, safe, soothed and secure) overrides the *exploratory system* (the innate drive to explore and learn about the world) (Siegel, 2012). Rose and Rogers (2012a) have suggested that early years professionals can focus attention on those elements considered crucial to the development of healthy attachments by envisaging themselves as both a secure base and a safe haven.

## Mindful Moment

### · The Key Person

A secure attachment with a Key Person provides young children with a secure base to *venture from* and playfully explore the environment, while the safe haven provides them with a *refuge* when that environment causes

> them any distress. In this way, the young child begins to negotiate the 'shifts between dependence, interdependence and independence' (Underwood, 2007: 48). The secure base/safe haven manifests itself for the child as both a physical and a psychological base and haven so that the child feels not just 'what it is to feel good physically' but also 'to be cherished emotionally' (McNamee et al., 2007: 280).
>
> In your work with children, how might you help a child to feel good physically and cherished emotionally? How do these ideas relate to the 4 S's of attachment considered earlier?

Siegel's work has shown how important connections between the limbic system and particular parts of the prefrontal cortex help to create nine key functions that are essential for health and well-being:

- bodily regulation – regulating the sympathetic and parasympathetic nervous systems;
- attuned communication – feeling felt and resonating with another;
- emotional balance – ability to self-regulate (good vagal tone);
- response flexibility – ability to pause before responding;
- fear modulation – inhibiting the fear response;
- empathy – to understand the internal state of another;
- insight – ability to perceive our own mind;
- moral awareness – behaviours for the social good;
- intuition – the wisdom of the body.

(Codrington, 2010: 293)

These functions, which operate within the frontal cortex, are critical for interpersonal signalling and effective social engagement, as well as helping to define the personality traits of a child (Schore, 2001a). These each contribute to our sense of belonging and our capacity for social connectedness and thus help to direct our social behaviour. The functioning of these various systems are largely a direct outcome of attachment relationships and their effectiveness is dependent upon how well our caregiver sees us, helps us to feel safe, soothes us when needed and establishes a sense of security in our early years. Our sense of safety is intricately linked to the regulation of our autonomic nervous system and the establishment of effective vagal tone. Optimal development occurs when the various systems involved in the attachment process effectively integrate together creating strong roadways (neural networks) which link all parts of the brain and body. This produces a brain, body and mind that is *well-integrated* (Siegel, 2012) – a key attribute in establishing well-being as noted earlier in this book.

We can see how some of the functions noted above begin to evolve through a consideration of the notion of *interactional synchrony*. The study of interactional synchrony is one of the key ways in which different researchers have attempted to explore the complex processes involved in the development of attachment relationships.

## Interactional synchrony

There are varying definitions of *interactional synchrony*. The notion was originally used to describe the way in which caregivers and infants appeared to imitate each other's actions and movements during interactions, such as facial expressions or speech patterns, so that they appeared to be in sync. For example, it was discovered that newborns synchronise their leg movements so that they mimic the rhythmic patterns of adult speech (Feldman, 2007). In this book, interactional synchrony is considered more broadly to refer to the *interpersonal relationship* between caregiver and child in which the caregiver sensitively *tunes into* the cared-for child in a responsive way which is in sync with the child's needs and interests. It is a mutually rewarding process for caregiver and child which helps to develop rapport, but most importantly helps the child to feel socially connected and develop a sense of belonging.

There is a wealth of consistent evidence which suggests that interactional synchrony between caregiver and young child plays a significant role in promoting later development such as attachment security, self-regulation, advanced language and the capacity for empathy (Feldman et al., 1999; Schore, 2001a). What lies at the root of this is a process referred to as *affect synchrony*. Affect synchrony helps to build the secure base/safe haven via responsive communication between caregiver and child. Berk refers to this as an 'emotional dance' in which 'the caregiver responds to infant signals in a well-timed, rhythmic, appropriate fashion' and in which the infant co-responds to the emotional state of the caregiver (2003: 422). Gerhardt articulates this further by calling it a 'mutual dance of responsiveness' (2004: 31). Interactions are thus *bi-directional* and *contingent* – in other words two-way and dependent upon each other. It is essentially two brains and two bodies, one mature and one immature, coordinating synchronised emotional communications. Siegel (2006) also highlights six important non-verbal aspects to what he calls contingent communication which include eye contact, facial expression, tone of voice, posture, gestures and the timing and intensity of the response – all physiologically based processes as we saw in Chapter 3. These are helpful mechanisms for practitioners to consider in relation to their own responses in their work with young children.

Interactional synchrony is a reciprocal process which is subtle and flexible and involves delicate tuning-in in order to develop a synchronous state of mutual connection and understanding. Thus part of the process of interactional synchrony involves the idea of *attunement*. Attunement develops via the series of synchronised, contingent sequences of interpersonal events or activities between caregiver and child. It entails an *attuned* dialogue between caregiver and child of sensory signals which can sometimes last only milliseconds. This dialogue oscillates between states of attention and inattention, engagement and disengagement, taking on a rhythmic structure which eventually become repetitive configurations or patterns of behaviour (Feldman, 2007). We can see a mature, advanced and overt manifestation of this in the turn-taking process that occurs in conversational dialogue when we meet a friend and talk about our weekend.

Drawing on the work of Winnicott (1971) and others, Underdown describes how attunement helps to create secure attachments through the 'empathetic responsiveness' of the caregiver (2007: 36). Being empathetically responsive means looking closely for verbal and non-verbal signals from the child that reflect how the child is feeling and what their needs and interests might be, and then making the necessary adjustments in terms of the mode, amount, variability and timing of the response. This creates what Schore (2001b) refers to as a reciprocal *psychophysiological state*. Such responsiveness might include recognising that when a child is being overstimulated the child might begin to cry, or that when he or she has become bored by a particular stimulus the child might look away. Siegel (2012) also refers to this process when he talks about tuning into whether a child is in a receptive or reactive state since this will affect the appropriate course of interaction. The signs or signals are not always obvious and may be expressed differently depending on the child. As practitioners, we can detect and learn from the signals given by the child and respond accordingly.

Some interesting correlations have been found between interactional synchrony and later development. For example, the matching of social gaze between caregiver and child correlates with social relatedness and cognitive growth (Feldman et al., 2011). In general, research suggests that synchrony between caregivers and three-month-old babies correlates with secure attachments at one year, lower behavioural problems at two years and an increased capacity for empathy at 13 years (Feldman, 2007). There also appears to be a correlation between interactional synchrony and better vagal tone (Moore and Calkins, 2004). Indeed, Feldman notes that 'biological rhythms provide the foundation for social rhythms' and highlights the evidence of how early syncronisation of physiological responses and rhythmic patterning creates the underpinning for lifelong social engagement and behaviours (2007: 342). Moreover, studies are suggesting that the synchrony of *psychobiological* states may help to create the foundation for the development of resilience (Ham and Tronick, 2006). You can read about this interesting link between rhythmic physiological processes and our emotional states in the case study below.

## Case Study

**Therapy interventions – establishing relationships through rhythmic connections**

An experienced therapist who utilises attachment-based interventions has found that even doing simple, repetitive rhythmic activities can make a contribution in building relationships at a physiological and emotional level. This patterning mimics the early processes of inter-actional synchrony necessary for the developing attachment relationship which is rooted in physiological responses to sensory stimulation. She writes:

> I had been asked by a local authority to work with a small group of their foster carers and their children (both fostered children and birth children). I decided to do a rhythmic activity called cup-dancing to relax the family and to ease communication. Cup-dancing is a cooperative game whereby a leader bangs a robust plastic cup in a repetitive rhythmic pattern which is copied by the rest of the group. It didn't take long for everyone to learn the rhythm and in no time we were drumming on the top of the beakers and using them to make a beat, passing a cup to the person on our right as we received one from the person on our left. It was a simple repetitive pattern but as the rhythm took hold, instead of watching their hands, parents and children began to engage each other's faces as they drummed and passed their cups. The session lasted only ten minutes and ended rather triumphantly, as the group increased the speed but held the rhythm.
>
> When I met up with the parents a couple of months later for a follow-up session, one of the parents told me that they had carried

on their cup dancing at home and their foster daughter had joined in. It became an after-school, pre-meal ritual with the family group developing variations on the cup dance theme. She commented that it seemed to be supporting a gradual shift to a more positive and rhythmic family dynamic. Their foster daughter seemed to be integrating better into the family, interrupting other people's conversations less and was calmer in the run-up to bedtime – which had previously been a time of conflict. (Clinical therapist)

## The Internal Working Model

As the infant internalises the experiences of the caregiving relationship, imprinting or neural coding takes place as the child starts to make sense of the world. In other words, strategies are encoded into the neural circuitry of the brain and linked to the physiological stress system in order to moderate feelings and regulate behaviour. It is the effective *integration* of these systems that Siegel (2012) considers to lie at the heart of well-being. While the biological function of attachment might be survival, the psychological function is to gain security (Schaffer, 2004). Over time, the cognitive representations or schema that are created out of children's repetitive, day-to-day experiences create a framework of neural networks or an *Internal Working Model*. The Internal Working Model essentially comprises stored memories of early interactions which eventually become *event scripts* and serve as a generalised *interpreter* of both the child's own and others' actions and behaviours. It also serves as a *predictor* and *filter* guiding the child's expectations about affective experiences. An infant who receives sufficiently consistent, responsive, attuned nurturing from his/her caregivers internalises their everyday, early interactions and experiences to create a *positive* Internal Working Model of memories. Positive Internal Working Models perceive relationships as generally affirming and worthwhile, view other people as generally available, trustworthy and dependable and, in turn, help to create a complementary model of the self as loveable, valuable and deserving of care (Bowlby, 1988).

Cultural influences such as a social group's informal norms about when, where and how one should express emotions (known as emotional display rules) will understandably affect the nature of the Internal Working Model (Berk, 2003), but universally it has been shown that caregiver responsiveness applies to all children, wherever they are born. This process is so powerful that caregiver attunement appears to play a more influential role in shaping children's personality than even innate temperament (Sroufe and Siegel, 2011). In other words, caregiver sensitivity seems to matter more than the easy or difficult temperament a child might have from birth (Schaffer, 1996). What much of the evidence suggests is that different early relational experiences create different Internal Working Models or attachment *types*.

## Attachment types

Attempts have been made to measure the nature of attachment and various *types* identified, which essentially differentiate between a *secure* and an *insecure* attachment (Ainsworth et al., 1978). The types identified were based on an experimental procedure known as the 'Strange Situation' designed to study the separation and reunion of an infant and mother under conditions of low and high stress. Different child behaviours were observed and categorised. Three categories of attachment pattern were established, with a fourth added later (Howe, 2011).

*Insecure* attachments arise when children have unmet attachment needs (Bergin and Bergin, 2009; Geddes, 2006). They appear to manifest themselves in various forms of *anxiety* (*avoidant, resistant* and *disorganised*), but their differences are best perceived as a 'continuum of security' rather than distinctive groups (Bergin and Bergin, 2009). Young children who develop an *anxious-avoidant* style of attachment have tended to have experienced insensitive, intrusive or rejecting caregiving. They end up seeking to meet their needs on their own, even when help might be advisable, as they have not been able to trust or rely on their caregiver. They may be task-orientated, self-reliant and high-achieving in some aspects, but can be generally socially uncomfortable, exhibit indifference and avoid close relationships. They may find it difficult to seek help, have limited creativity and may be prone to sudden outbursts. Young children who have an *anxious-ambivalent* style of attachment tend to have experienced inconsistent and largely unresponsive caregiving. They are easily frustrated and may present as both clingy or rejecting of a practitioner as they seek both comfort from, but are unable to be comforted by, adults. They may appear cooperative and compliant, but also present as immature, fussy, helpless, passive or whiney, or they may be angry or petulant. They may also present as attention-seeking, hyperactive and have difficulty recovering from upset (Bergin and Bergin, 2009; Geddes, 2006).

*Anxious-disorganised* children are usually from neglected, abusive and/or chaotic homes. The child may feel confused by practitioners and experience them as frightening or frightened. These children are often highly vigilant, easily distracted, have a strong sense of fear, panic, or helplessness, and may present with bizarre, extreme, unpredictable or distressing behaviour, which adults may find shocking and difficult to manage. They often present as sensitive to criticism, defiant and/or controlling and are easily overwhelmed (Bergin and Bergin, 2009; Geddes, 2006).

The complexities of these different forms of insecure attachments make diagnosis difficult, particularly as they are susceptible to cultural variations and are based on an experimental procedure (Berk, 2003). Children can also display different attachment patterns with different caregivers. There is only one medical diagnosis of an attachment disorder, namely *reactive attachment disorder*, which invariably arises from a disorganised form of attachment (Hornor, 2008). Practitioners should be cautious in making their own informal generalised diagnoses of unmet attachment needs but be sensitive to the possibility that they are likely to encounter children with different Internal Working Models that have evolved as an adaptation to particular emotional climates of early caregiving.

## Mindful Moment

You can find out more about the Strange Situation and different attachment types by going on YouTube and watching a clip produced by the New York Attachment Consortium at: https://www.youtube.com/watch?v=PnFKaaOSPmk&list=PLF4764363FAE09F64&index=2.

This clip shows how Mary Ainsworth attempted to classify the different ways in which children attach to their caregivers depending upon their style of interaction.

Watch the clip and think about its implications for your practice. What does it tell you about children's needs and how adults should respond? (Note that ethical concerns have been raised about this experimental procedure.)

Can you think of alternative ways of ascertaining young children's attachment types without putting them through such a deliberately stressful situation?

# Secure attachments and the implications for practice

In the early chapters, we saw how the brain develops sequentially and how this development is rooted in the stress response system which helps to organise and regulate the more advanced thinking parts of the brain. From a neurological perspective, differences have been found in brain functioning between different attachment types. For example, disorganised attachments show more amygdala dysfunction and immaturity in the limbic-autonomic network of the brain (Schore, 2014). Evidence shows that children who are neglected develop particular biochemical reactions that are rooted in the amygdala and mediated by the frontal cortex (Perry, 2006; Gerhardt, 2004). Another recent study using new technology has demonstrated the key role played by the amygdala in mediating autonomic activity related with human attachment security. This study has added to other evidence which shows how insecure attachments create a heightened sympathetic nervous system activity, such as increased heart rate and increase in cortisol secretion (Lemche et al., 2006).

In contrast, the neurodevelopment of securely attached children creates positive Internal Working Models (Fivush, 2006). Securely attached children are more able to trust and rely on practitioners, are more confident in forming meaningful relationships, make the most of their learning opportunities, engage in more productive activities, problem-solve and explore the wider world (Bergin and Bergin, 2009). Moreover, securely attached children are better at emotion regulation and have lower negative emotionality, higher empathy and greater resilience (Panfile and Laible, 2012). Thus, if a child is unable to rely on an adult to respond to their needs in times of stress, they are unable to learn how to soothe themselves, manage their emotions and engage in reciprocal relationships. A child's initial dependence on others for protection provides the experiences and skills to help a child cope with frustrations and develop self-confidence and pro-social relationships – all qualities necessary to promote positive engagement with learning. Indeed, research has inextricably linked attachment to school readiness and school success (Commodari, 2013).

Therefore a key message for practitioners is that the nature of the attachment type can predict emotional responses and social behaviour. It also can affect a child's capacity for optimal learning (Geddes, 2006). An awareness of attachment difficulties has important implications for practitioners given that between a third and a quarter of children may be insecurely attached (Bergin and Bergin, 2009). It is therefore likely that all early years practitioners will encounter at least some children within their professional context who have unmet attachment needs with a subsequent effect on the child's behaviour and learning. Of additional significance is the evidence which reveals the *compensatory* role affectional ties can provide to help counteract poor attachments, highlighting the role of the early years practitioner in providing a *buffer zone* for young children regardless of their parental relationships (Berk, 2003). As we saw earlier, this is epitomised in the role of the Key Person within the Early Years Foundation Stage statutory curriculum in England (DfE, 2014a). The importance of this role is illustrated in the following case study.

## Case Study

### The Key Person

The following tells the story of a three-year-old boy who started at a nursery and how the Key Person worked hard in building a relationship with the child, particularly taking into account his emotional needs. This helped to address the insecurities he felt in transitioning from the home to pre-school.

Alan started at his local pre-school when he was three years old. At the pre-school, he did not initiate conversations very much but did not appear to be unduly unhappy. His sensitive Key Person took care to ensure he felt seen, safe, soothed and secure. The practitioner also spent time closely observing Alan to ascertain his play interests and noticed that he spent most of the day tightly clenching his fists together. This meant that he was unable to participate in many of the activities. The sensitive practitioner decided to investigate this further and after discussing the matter with the boy's mother, she discovered that the mother had decided Alan was now too grown up to have his comfort blanket and had taken it away. The Key Person considered that Alan's fist clenching was his attempt to hold onto his invisible comfort blanket during the stressful transition to a new environment full of novel experiences. Alan was imagining his blanket was still there to comfort him. As a result, a new comfort blanket was purchased and this transitional object (as Winnicott (1971) called such items), alongside the Key Person, helped to sooth Alan and create a bridge as he adjusted to his new context. As time went on, Alan developed an attachment to his Key Person, became less reliant on the comfort blanket and started to feel more safe and secure in the pre-school, enabling him to engage his exploratory system to learn from his enabling environment hands free!

In the next chapter we will see how nurturing attachments create the groundwork for emotional self-regulation.

---

## Key Points

- A secure attachment to a warm, responsive, consistent caregiver creates a fundamental basis for lifelong health and well-being.
- Attachment can be understood via the 4 S's model – children need to feel seen, safe, soothed and secure.
- Much of the attachment relationship hinges upon a caregiver's capacity to develop interactional synchrony with a child.
- Early interactions develop significant neural connections within the brain and form the basis for effective stress regulation, creating the Internal Working Model.
- Different attachment styles arise based on the emotional climate of the caregiving environment.
- Young children can develop secondary attachments to early years practitioners which will foster their health and well-being.

---

## Useful Further Reading and Websites

- Elfer, P., Goldsmied, E. and Selleck, D. (2012) *Key Persons in the Early Years: Building Relationships for Quality Provision in Early Years Settings and Schools*. London: Routledge. This book provides an essential review of the role of the Key Person.
- Bergin, C. and Bergin, D. (2009) 'Attachment in the classroom', *Educational Psychology Review*, 21: 141–70. This provides a useful summary of attachment theory.
- This website focuses on the application of attachment theory to schools but is still relevant for early years contexts at: http://attachmentaware schools.com/.
- The International Attachment Network has its own website which contains further information and training on attachment at: http://ian-attachment.org.uk/.

# CHAPTER 6

# EMOTIONAL DEVELOPMENT AND REGULATION

---

## Chapter Overview

This chapter builds on the previous chapter which considered the fundamental importance of nurturing relationships in the early years. The two chapters are best read together as they complement each other. In this chapter, we look more closely at the *emotional* brain and how attachment relationships help young children's emotional development, particularly their capacity to regulate their emotions and behaviour. It draws attention to the role of empathy in emotional regulation and the development of what is known as *Theory of Mind* and *emotional intelligence*. It also considers the process of *reflective functioning* which links closely to the notion of *interactional synchrony* that was outlined in the previous chapter. Although this book does not specifically address social development, the implications of children's capacity to self-regulate and develop emotional intelligence for social interactions and behaviour is implied.

---

## The emotional brain

What has become apparent from attachment and attachment-related studies is how young children receive sensory stimuli at a perceptual level (neuroception) within the limbic system, particularly in the amygdala. Initially, the early maturing amygdala acts as a sensory gateway to the limbic system and drives the primary behaviours of the newborn, invariably expressed in the form of crying. Life experiences eventually create neural connections between the limbic system and the cortex to create the thinking emotional brain. In optimal contexts, the frontal cortex can eventually take on a stronger control over the functions provided by the flight/fight response, so that the child can adapt to the complexity of life's challenges and mediate responses accordingly.

Put simply, the secure attachment relationship can help to build a system that supports moderation of the survival-based flight/fight response when necessary – in other words, *override* the *override*. The integrated system becomes the executive of stress regulation (Schore, 2001b). These neural networks of the *thinking emotional brain* thus monitor, adjust and correct emotional responses and behaviour according to context, and later link emotional perceptions to more explicit cognitive understanding (Schore, 2001a). Thus emotional development (and therefore cognitive development) depends on communication between the autonomic nervous system and the brain as sensory, physiological states are conveyed to the brain, which in turn conveys information back to the autonomic nervous system to moderate responses. This process becomes increasingly more complex as the child encounters more life experiences and emotional brain circuitry begins to feed into more rational cognitive processing. Part of this progression involves the development of a *Theory of Mind* which is discussed later in this chapter.

Schore (2001a) suggests that early development of the emotional brain is of particular significance for the quality of lifespan development. What is particularly interesting about this research is the suggestion that processing in the emotional brain of sensory cues such as facial expressions (neuroception) occurs not only faster but more unconsciously than in the conscious 'thinking' areas of the cortex. Therefore we perceive information in, for example, tone of voice in the emotional parts of the brain and begin to respond accordingly *before* conscious awareness. Schore also explains how the emotional brain plays a superior role in regulating not just our emotional, social and behavioural reactions, but also our physiological responses such as vagal tone and our stress response system. This part of our brain develops sequentially from the lower, more primitive parts of the brain before extending into the upper parts of our brain where more advanced symbolic thinking develops, such as learning to talk. This *neurosequencing* process emerges out of our attachment relationships and the more secure the attachment relationship, the more efficiently the emotional brain will regulate our health and well-being (Schore, 2001a). He writes:

> Early emotionally laden attachment experiences indelibly impact and
> alter the early developing . . . brain, which for the rest of the lifespan
> is dominant for the non-verbal, holistic, spontaneous (unconscious)

processing of emotional information and social interactions, for enabling the organism to regulate affect and cope with stresses and challenges, and thereby for emotional resilience and emotional well-being in later stages of life. (2014: 1)

As we have cautioned elsewhere in this book, we need to be careful of oversimplifying and over-interpreting findings from the neurosciences (Rose and Abi-Rached, 2013). Nonetheless, Schore (2001a, 2014) draws attention to the well-established evidence that attachment interactions literally programme the developing brain, particularly in the first two years of life. The wiring that occurs through interpersonal exchanges affects a child's affiliation for social connectiveness, interdependence and emotional growth, including stress regulation. Responding effectively to a crying baby, for example, helps to moderate the release of the stress hormone cortisol, the release of which is triggered when the baby has an unmet need. Too much cortisol release has been shown to inhibit brain development (Entwistle, 2013) and Chapter 3 has highlighted the traumatic effect of stress on the brain. This process has been referred to as *imprinting* (Schore, 2014) and was first articulated by Bowlby when he theorised that infants develop a biological control system to help regulate the limbic system and which formulates the Internal Working Model as discussed in the previous chapter.

# Emotional development and the path to emotional regulation

A key aspect in the process of developing positive Internal Working Models appears to lie within the rhythmic patterning of attunement and interactional synchrony. Within this process, a child's developing sense of how to regulate their emotions plays a pivotal part. *Emotional regulation* essentially involves the capacity to monitor or adjust the duration or intensity of an emotional reaction to a more balanced and comfortable level in order to ensure a constructive resolution to a stressful event or to achieve a goal productively (Eisenberg and Fabes, 1995). Gross (2013) interprets this in terms of either *up-regulating* or *down-regulating* the intensity or duration of an emotional response. This is a complex process that involves accommodating an increasing array of emotional states. In Chapter 1, we saw how it is considered that we are born with what are termed *primary* emotions (Berk, 2003). These are the emotions of joy, surprise, interest, fear, anger, sadness and disgust. By about the age of two, *secondary* or 'self-conscious' emotions emerge such as pride, envy, guilt and shame, although the development of these secondary (also known as higher-order feelings) are far more *culturally dependent* (Sander, 2013).

Emotions are both a physical and a mental experience and manifest in different behaviours. By the time we reach adulthood, our brains have woven together a complex circuitry involving many parts of the brain, but they are all rooted in and built from the primary emotions of the limbic system, whose primary responsibility is to regulate our survival. The neurologist Damasio (1994) has shown how emotions fundamentally underpin all rational behaviour, so much so that without emotional expression, all reasonable thinking and memory formation is not possible. In turn, emotions are essentially a direct expression of underlying biological regulatory processes (Damasio, 1998). What has become clear from studies about emotion is that they are intricately linked to our survival both physically and socially, creating a complex web of emotions related to, for example, social engagement, sense of self, learning and morality (Sander, 2013). They therefore provide an essential *function* in our health and well-being.

We appear to have evolved two different systems to help achieve our survival which utilise negative and positive emotions (Music, 2011). Negative emotions (such as fear and anger) appear to exist to ensure security and safety – known as the *defensive* system – while positive emotions (such as joy and interest) operate to enable us to explore the world – known as the *appetitive* system. These two systems create conditions where our behaviour can express itself in an *approach/appetite/interest* mode and an *avoidance/aversion/withdrawal* mode (Damasio, 1998; Sander, 2013). Some research on the links between emotional states and physical health show that positive emotions help to create healthier patterns of physiological functioning within, for example, cardiovascular activity and the immune system. Excessive negative emotions, unsurprisingly, are associated with unhealthy patterns of physiological functioning (Salovey et al., 2000).

Music makes the important point that these two systems are not necessarily polar opposites and the presence of one feeling does not necessarily negate the presence of the opposite feeling. He notes that 'the absence of happiness is different from the presence of unhappiness' and that people who are generally more positive do not necessarily experience less negative feelings (2011: 212). It is possible, for example, to feel both good and bad about the same event or person – to love someone but to also feel annoyed by them. This is borne out by the fact that positive and negative emotions appear to be processed differently by the brain and the body.

Pain and reward, for example, are processed via different parts of the brain (Sander, 2013). It also appears that our brains are more sensitive and pay more heed to our negative emotions. This is not surprising given that our negative emotions enable us to respond to threats, actual or perceived. There is some interesting research that shows in order to feel satisfied in our relationships, we need six times more positive interactions to occur for every negative interaction (Gottman, 1994).

There is now a wealth of growing research and literature on the power of positive emotions (for example, Seligman, 2003), but as we have seen we must be careful not to oversimplify the complexity of our emotional development. What appears to be of particular importance for mental health is the need to experience *joyful* experiences alongside a capacity to cope with and regulate our stressful experiences. We know that feeling happy is linked to a range of benefits related to our health, well-being and learning (Schoffham and Barnes, 2011), but integral to this is *self-regulation* and this journey begins in our early relationships and the support we are given.

# Managing stressful encounters and misattunement

The previous chapter emphasised the importance of attunement and synchronicity between caregiver and child. It is also important to recognise that this match is never completely perfect and that mismatches can and will occur. Stern (2002: 133) referred to these as 'missteps in the dance'. Misattunements will occur naturally as the caregiver adjusts to the temperament and particularities of the infant and vice versa. They will also occur due to the normal demands of life that might interfere with a caregiver's capacity to respond at the right time and in the right way to a child. They are also necessary in order to enable the child to begin to take on their own self-regulation or to learn social rules (Badenoch, 2008). Fortunately, our systems are receptive to, and can accommodate, relatively small stresses. Indeed, stress itself is *needed* in order to learn how to *overcome* it. The *key* to the process appears to be that mismatches can become increasingly tolerable for the child as long as they are packaged in manageable bundles and sufficiently co-regulated during the earliest period of development. Indeed, adjustment to not having needs met is an important life lesson for young children and links to the idea of children beginning to learn that they can cope and change their own circumstances, developing a sense of their own agency and resilience (as we will see in later chapters). Perfection is therefore not necessary and we need only be a *good enough* caregiver (Winnicott, 1973), but remember that being *good enough* does not mean taking on a minimalist stance. We should still be driven by the need to establish interactional synchronicity responding in a timely and effective manner, such as looking out for cues from the child when they need a break from stimulation or require to be proactively soothed. In this way, we can avoid too much unnecessary mismatching. Moreover, re-attunement or *repair* is essential when misattunement or *rupture* occurs (Siegel, 2012). In Chapter 11 we will consider the impact of trauma on young children which invariably occurs when children are not helped to overcome their stress and reparation does not occur.

## Mindful Moment

What circumstances might lead to a mismatch in your own practice in the quality of the connection you have with children, such as when and how you are able to meet a child's needs?

# Emotional self-regulation and reflective functioning

Infants, in particular, are experiencing primary emotions for the first time and thus operate on an emotional rollercoaster with few controls for steering or moderating the ride. With time, their experiences of emotions become tempered by the attuned and nurturing caregiver who is able to support the child on their journey to self-regulation. Infants who have caregivers who are appropriately responsive to their emotional cues are less fussy, more easily soothed and have an increased desire for playful exploration (Berk, 2003). What seems to be of particular importance is the need to help children to *contain* their feelings as young children's immature neural circuits are not well-equipped to cope with either too much positive or negative emotion. For example, smiling at a baby stimulates the child via the release of biochemicals which help the brain to grow, but if this interaction becomes too arousing for the child, the caregiver needs to moderate the response (Schore, 2001b).

Invariably, it is negative circumstances that cause the young child to become more easily overwhelmed since these are usually rooted in the need for immediate survival. The containment process can manifest itself in both physical form (being cuddled) and emotionally (having feelings noticed, accepted, understood and soothed) (Bion, 1967). *Containment* enables a child to feel that they are being held in the mind and body of the caregiver (Winnicott, 1971). It requires the adult to undertake a process of what is termed *mentalisation* (Fonagy et al., 2004). In other words, the capacity to understand the child's inner 'mental states' based on their needs and feelings and to interpret their behaviour. Siegel describes a similar process via his concept of *mindsight*. As Meins (1999) shows, the caregiver does not just seek to understand what a child is thinking and feeling but also 'shares' this with them and reflects it back to them (which she calls mind-mindedness). In this way, a caregiver effectively helps to *translate* or *digest* the overwhelming experience for the child until they learn to do it for themselves. This helps the child to develop *self-awareness* of their own inner thoughts and feelings which lay the foundation for a sense of self.

However, we need to do more than just monitor and articulate a child's signals, we need to examine our *own reactions*. This is known as *reflecting functioning* and is essentially our ability to monitor and tune into not just a child's internal signals, but also our own internal state. In doing so, we can regulate our own arousal levels and hence a child's, adjusting both the type and intensity of the response accordingly (Schore, 2001a). As the NSPCC notes, 'a mother's reflective skills determine whether her child learns from her by default or by design' (NSPCC, 2011). It is a dynamic and ongoing process which helps to establish interactive synchrony and build a child's internal working model. This idea of adapting our interactions to suit the child's needs via reflective functioning is explored throughout this book.

Goleman (1995) has shown how *emotional learning* occurs more readily during the first three or four years than in later life. Thus, although the cultural context plays a role in the development of emotions, the practitioner's role in supporting infants' and young children's regulation of all their emotions (both primary and secondary) remains critical. This is because, firstly, the infant is so dependent on the caregiver for help in managing the more primary emotions and, secondly, because cultural expectations and feedback help to determine the nature and intensity of the secondary emotions. As LeDoux puts it, 'we come into the world capable of being afraid and capable of being happy, but we must learn which things make us afraid and which make us happy' (cited in Geake, 2009: 116).

## Mindful Moment

Arnold et al. (2010) in their work on schema development at the Pen Green Centre in England have been exploring how young children represent their emotional worlds. Drawing on attachment theory and the work of Winnicott and others, their research on children's schemas (mental representations and their behavioural manifestations) has shown how young children use schemas 'for comfort, to give form to, and to explore and begin to understand complex life events and changes' (Arnold et al., 2010: 11). For example, they illustrate how children coping with the loss of a grandparent might express and come to terms with this by *containing* objects inside other objects, symbolising the notion of here and gone. Such actions enable children to mentalise or reflect on experiences either as a source of comfort, expression or to 'work through' the emotional experience in order to make sense of it. Although we need to be careful not to over-interpret all children's actions as a reflection of emotional events, nonetheless this work does appear to resonate with other research and theory on children's emotional development and links to therapeutic interventions, such as Theraplay, which utilise play experiences to support the recovery of traumatised children (see the case study in Chapter 11).

# Empathy and Theory of Mind

Attachment security has been shown to predict a greater capacity for empathy (Panfile and Laible, 2012). Empathy involves a complex interaction of cognition and affect. It includes the ability to detect different emotions and to take on another person's perspective, but more than that, it includes the ability to *'feel with* that person, or respond emotionally in a similar way' (Berk, 2003: 407). In the early years, we need to help support young children's attunement to emotions since 'the root of caring stems from the capacity of empathy' (Goleman, 1995: 96) and can be encouraged by building self-awareness, which in turn builds skills in reading others' emotions. Moreover, higher moral reasoning is also associated with empathy (Panfile and Laible, 2012).

Empathy is inextricably linked to children developing a *Theory of Mind*. This is the ability to recognise and understand that others have beliefs, views and intentions that are different from your own. Put simply, it is the capacity to put yourself in someone else's shoes and relies on social experiences to help bring it to fruition. Theory of Mind is also known as mentalising (which we mentioned earlier), but Baron-Cohen offers a more familiar term – empathising (Blakemore and Frith, 2005) (although Theory of Mind involves both cognitive and affective elements). Some research suggests that it is not until children are about four years of age that they have an established Theory of Mind, but neuroscientific evidence reveals the existence of *mirror neurons* which can be activated in our brains from a very early age (see Chapter 2). This remarkable finding shows that even when we are unable to perform an action ourselves, our brain can still mimic the action internally. Further research has shown similar activation when we watch someone getting hurt – our mirror neurons activate a similar response in our brain even though we might not be physically hurt (Music, 2011). It is now believed that these mirror neurons appear to play a role in developing empathy and more effective socialising by enabling us to read others' minds (Blakemore and Frith, 2005) – in other words, to develop a *Theory of Mind*. We know, for example, that a child as young as one can feel distress when she sees another child cry, challenging the egocentric perspective held by Piaget and others that young children are unable to view the world from another perspective (Goleman, 1995).

The ability to empathise with others has important consequences for how children interact socially and develop their own relationships. When interacting with their peers, young children need to employ *affective synchrony*, largely at a subconscious level, to read and interpret others' behaviour and intentions (Schore, 2014). The ability to empathically resonate with others' emotional states, to communicate their own emotional states and to regulate interpersonal exchanges are important foundations for pro-social behaviour. This includes being able to cope during stressful encounters such as the novelty of starting nursery or having to share toys with others. Indeed, most of life's challenges involve managing the transition of changing in response to environmental pressures, while accommodating our innate desire for stability and continuity (Schore, 2001a). Moreover, clear links have been found between a child's empathic responses for others' distress in inhibiting aggressive behaviour and in helping to establish pro-social and moral behaviour (Panfile and Laible, 2012). Role modelling by adults plays an important part in the development of *empathic scripts* for young children's Internal Working Model. We will see in Chapter 8 how Emotion Coaching can help to develop such empathic scripts.

Theory of Mind starts to emerge as the child shifts from unconscious brain dominance to more conscious brain functioning in the second year. This enables the child to begin to utilise other mechanisms such as language and sequencing to help with the management of self-regulation

(Schore, 2001a). Left and right brain hemisphere integration occurs through the corpus callosum, for example in the translation of feelings into words. Our capacity to regulate our emotions forms the roots of what has been termed *emotional intelligence*.

---

### Mindful Moment

In this section, we noted Schore's (2001a) point that most of life's challenges involve managing the transition of changing in response to environmental pressures while accommodating our innate desire for stability and continuity.

Think about this in relation to your own experiences – for example, can you think of a time when you had to change something but struggled and resisted it? How did you overcome this and regain a status quo?

---

# Emotional intelligence

The term emotional intelligence was first coined by Salovey and Meyer who later defined it as:

> The ability to perceive accurately, appraise, and express emotion; the ability to access and/or generate feelings when they facilitate thought; the ability to understand emotion and emotional knowledge; and the ability to regulate emotions to promote emotional and intellectual growth (1990: 10).

Goleman highlights how the term emotion is derived from the Latin verb to move emphasising that emotions 'are, in essence, impulses to act' (1995: 6). Goleman's work acknowledges the role of the emotional mind in feeding into and informing the operations of the rational mind. The rational mind can refine and sometimes veto the input of the impulsive emotional mind *but only if it learns to do this*. We saw earlier how we need to develop systems that enable us to override the override to prevent what Goleman (1995) refers to as *emotional hijacking*.

We now know that the same neural pathways are used for both an actual experience and the remembrance of an event and that 'endangerment can be signalled not just by an outright physical threat but also, as is more often the case, by a symbolic threat to self-esteem or dignity: being treated unjustly or rudely, being insulted or demeaned, being frustrated in pursuing an important goal' (Goleman, 1995: 60). In the Western world, we no longer live in a society in which danger is ever present, or at least it takes on different forms than an immediately life-threatening situation (for the most part). Therefore the role of those parts of the brain which provide a more analytic and appropriate response to perceived danger become more pertinent to allow for greater discernment in emotional responses and subsequent behaviour. These ideas were first considered in the first three chapters and are explored again in relation to resilience in Chapter 9. Emotional intelligence is also considered to correlate with positive physical health and thus forms an integral part in promoting health and well-being (Salovey et al., 2000).

## Case Study

### Improving emotional well-being

An educational psychologist who works closely with teachers and teaching assistants to support young children in schools here provides an example of working with a six-year-old boy who had been diagnosed with Autism Spectrum Disorder (ASD) and was selectively mute (chose not to speak) at school. She used a process called video self-modelling (VSM) to support his emotional well-being which led to academic progress.

Five-year-old James often did not complete tasks and displayed much anxiety as well as not speaking or interacting with other children in any way. The educational psychologist suggested VSM which derives from the work of Albert Bandura's social learning theory (1977) and the role of observational learning in helping children to acquire skills through imitation. Observational learning can encourage and develop young people's self-efficacy, including their beliefs about their ability to complete tasks and reach goals.

The intervention involved filming James. He was happy to read out loud, so videos were made with him reading out basic phrases that he might say in the classroom. From the beginning, James loved watching himself on video. It was noticeable that he took note of his performance and strove to improve his next video. He was also videoed talking with another boy and during this rehearsed interaction he asked his friend to play with him and to sit next to him at lunchtime.

*(Continued)*

*(Continued)*

After one week James's face became more animated, he was smiling in class and interacting non-verbally with other children. At the end of week two, James was starting to communicate verbally, such as answering questions during circle time. After one month, James's communications with the teacher and other children improved significantly, as did his school work and social activities with other children. His improved well-being was apparent to all.

(Licette, educational psychologist)

## Key Points

- The emotional brain and emotional development is integral to the maturation of the rational mind.
- Emotional and behavioural self-regulation develops over time, largely through attachment relationships and via integrated systems in the brain and body.
- Nurturing role modelling promotes the development of empathy which supports pro-social behaviours and a theory of mind.
- Reflective functioning by the adult helps to establish attunement and interactional synchrony, supporting a child's self-awareness.
- Emotional intelligence evolves in response to the increasingly complex environment and plays a key role in regulating health and well-being.

# Useful Further Reading and Websites

- Gerhardt, S. (2004) *Why Love Matters: How Affection Shapes a Baby's Brain*. London: Routledge. This book provides an accessible insight into some of the neuroscientific explanations of how loving relationships in the early years foster emotional health.
- Arnold, C. and the Pen Green Team (2010) *Understanding Schemas and Emotion in Early Childhood*. London: Sage. This book provides a valuable and practical insight into how young children represent their emotional worlds.
- Have a look at Daniel Goleman's website which has some useful resources about emotional intelligence at: http://www.danielgoleman.info/.

# CHAPTER 7

# ACTIVE LEARNING

---

## Chapter Overview

This chapter focuses on the significance of active learning and considers the role of play in promoting psychomotor and cognitive development and how these are stimulated by physical activity and active and interactive learning. The processes of equilibration and self-regulation in absorbing new learning through sensorimotor experiences and sensory integration are reviewed. The role of schemes such as Fundamental Movement Skills (FMS) and Forest Schools will be considered in relation to early years practitioners providing opportunities for the development of motor and coordination skills.

---

## What is meant by active learning?

Active learning is open to many interpretations. Piaget (1954) considered that children learnt best through *doing* and *actively* exploring the world around them – discovery or experiential learning – which enables actively constructing knowledge through interaction with the environment. Halpenny and Pettersen (2014) outline Piaget's constructivist approach as containing three elements: *active, progressive* and *constructive*. It is the *active* part that is fundamental for our growth and development. Knowledge is not simply given to us from external sources; we act upon the information we receive, process it and interpret it to make sense of the situation. For example, a young child may be given a rattle-type toy and the parent shows the child how to shake the rattle to make a noise. The child may imitate this and replicate what they have observed. Left to their own devices they may then experiment with the toy: they might wave it around, bang it on different surfaces to see what noise it makes, drop it on the floor, bite it, suck it, chew it and even throw it. All the while they are acting upon it and learning about its properties and their exploration of what it is and what it can do is creatively driven. They are actively participating in the learning that takes place.

In England, the Early Years Foundation Stage (EYFS) perceives active learning in terms of motivational learning and resilience. It refers to active learning in relation to children's ability to 'concentrate and keep on trying if they encounter difficulties, and enjoy achievements' (DfE, 2014a). The idea of active learning within the EYFS is also encompassed as a key characteristic of effective learning – *playing and exploring,* which emphasises young children's investigation and experience of the environment and 'having a go' in true Piagetian tradition. Another characteristic of effective learning focuses on cognitive aspects of children's development and how children develop and create ideas and thinking strategies. Moylett refers to these characteristics as the *skill, will* and *thrill* of learning – 'the *skill* to get engaged, the *will* to keep going and the *thrill* of discovery' (2013: 1). The focus on play is emphasised as a medium of learning for children to 'develop the skills they need in order to become good learners – [to] . . . develop flexibility of thought, build their confidence and see problems from different perspectives' (Tickell, 2011: 3).

## What are the benefits of active learning?

There are two key strands to active learning: one strand is the *child's role and participation* in their own learning and the need to empower children so that they take an 'active' role in their own learning and understand that they can make changes to their lives (Vickery, 2014). Therefore, the learning that takes place becomes more meaningful to them. The second strand considers the *physical* aspects of active learning and the development of gross and fine motor skills, including balancing and displaying physical skills and dexterity. Sensory experience and integration are central to this. Moreover, exercise and the importance of establishing healthy lifestyles and habits from an early age form an important part of active learning and its role in the promotion of health and well-being.

1. The key benefits of active learning in respect of *children participating in their own learning* are that it:

   - empowers the child to be an active participant in their own learning and take control of their own learning;
   - raises confidence and self-esteem by developing a sense of achievement;
   - develops strategic awareness;
   - stimulates creativity in learning through opportunities to utilise their imagination and creative abilities.

2. The key benefits of active learning with a focus on the *physical aspects of development* are:

   - exercise;
   - establishing healthy lifestyle habits;
   - developing anti-obesity strategies;
   - enabling physical development of limbs, lungs, coordination, balance and physical dexterity;
   - aiding schema creation (patterns of thought and action) and practising and mastering skills;
   - helping interpretation of sensory information;
   - fostering incidental learning such as learning social rules and sharing;
   - raising self-esteem by developing a sense of achievement in acquiring physical skills and attaining goals.

## Learning through play

All mammals engage in play. Parker-Rees (2010) states that play activity among species correlates with the size of their brains – the more play, the bigger the brain. There is a wealth of literature on play which has identified the value of play as a medium for development and learning (Wood and Attfield, 2005; Moyles, 2015). There are many debates about the nature of play, including whether it ought to be viewed as a vehicle for learning (Rogers, 2011), but this chapter highlights the natural and essential opportunities provided by play for young children's health and well-being. There is also the sheer enjoyment factor which creates a value in itself for promoting play. Play manifests itself in many different forms such as sensorimotor, constructive, symbolic, socio-dramatic and rule-bound play (Macintyre, 2012). Play can be categorised according to the developmental opportunities it provides: cognitive or intellectual play, linguistic play, social and emotional play and psychomotor or physical play. Vygotsky suggested that play promotes social and emotional self-regulation as children restrain their impulses by following social rules and enact social-cultural roles through their play (Bodrova and Leong, 2011). Play can also be used therapeutically to support traumatised children. The playful, inter-active games between caregiver and infant, like peekaboo and finger rhymes, help the child begin the journey towards linguistic competence. It is clear that these developmental categories overlap. Nonetheless, while endorsing a holistic perspective and acknowledging that all learning is integrated, this chapter focuses primarily on the *physical* act of play and how it affects *psychomotor* and *cognitive* development.

## Mindful Moment

Analyse what learning and development took place through playing with a favourite toy or game when you were younger. You might consider the key areas:

- cognitive/thinking/intellectual
- social and emotional
- linguistic
- physical.

# Physical play and early psychomotor development

Psychomotor development refers to the growth of coordination and integration between our body and brain, between our physical move-ments and our cognitive understanding (Goddard-Blythe, 2008). Human beings are designed for physical activity which is essential for healthy growth and development. From the outset infants are active partici-pants in their own learning. Their initial reflexes provide a platform for the development of sensorimotor skills that ensure their survival. The newborn (neonate) is born relatively helpless in comparison with other mammals but has certain reflex responses designed to ensure survival (many of which first appear in the womb). These primitive or primary reflexes include reflexes for feeding (*sucking* and *rooting* reflexes) and *grasping* (the Palmer reflex) (Shaffer, 1999). The *startle* or Moro reflex is an instinctive response to unexpected events such as a loud noise and links closely to our flight/flight response. Some reflexes are present at birth then disappear as part of normal neurological development as the brain matures (particularly the cerebellum) in response to physical interaction with the environment. With repetition, the reflexes are increasingly replaced with voluntary movements and become integrated with the sensory system. Goddard-Blythe (2008) highlights some interesting research which suggests that developmental difficulties, such as poor coordination and fine motor skill development, may lie in the retention of primary reflexes and/or poor integration of all the different sensory systems.

Since neonates are relatively helpless, they quickly learn to develop *proximity-promoting* behaviours which elicit adult responses and assistance to ensure their survival, such as crying and smiling. Smiling is a strong social signal for maintaining contact with carers (Izard, 1982). Crying is the baby's way of communicating its needs. The earliest cries from babies are *unlearned* and *involuntary* responses to indicate that something is wrong (Shaffer, 1999). The cries are distress signals to alert the caregiver that they need attention. This demonstrates that babies are already active players in 'manipulating' their environment.

These behaviours are part of the process of attachment explored in Chapter 5 and reflect both *attractive* attachment behaviours (such as smiling) and *aversive* attachment behaviours (such as crying). As their ability to move and explore increases, their proximity-promoting behaviours become more complex *proximity-seeking* behaviours (such as crawling towards a caregiver). Young children who are eventually able to *balance* their proximity behaviours (a need to return to the *safe haven*) with their exploratory behaviours (setting out to explore from the *secure base*) are often those who are securely attached (Ainsworth, 1979). These behaviours are all part of developing social interaction and learning how their actions can change the behaviour of those around them. As they develop further, they become skilled in interacting with people and the environment and in doing so they learn about the world around them.

# Developmental progress

Motor skills become more intricate as the child develops and acquires the ability to balance and coordinate: *locomotor* (moving movement like crawling), *non-locomotor* (stationary movement like bending) and *manipulative* (dexterous movement) like throwing balls. There is clear progression in terms of increasing complexity and maturity, but there are debates about the usefulness of developmental milestones and stages of development in the early years which largely centre around understandable concerns about developmental delay or political drivers such as *school readiness* which affect expectations about what young children could or should be doing (Whitebread and Bingham, 2012). The political and economic drive to intervene early to help address potential problems is considered in later chapters. Rose and Rogers (2012a), drawing on Thomas (2008), note the dilemma for practitioners in using milestones to recognise possible developmental delay. Practitioners need some understanding of so-called typical development in order to ascertain an atypical need which may require additional support. However, having milestones that are too broad and overlapping make it difficult for judgements to be made or misjudgements may occur as emerging skills are assessed too soon. This means we need a balance between being 'both inactive and vigilant at the same time' (Rose and Rogers, 2012a: 114).

As children's physical capability continues to develop they utilise *fine motor skills* such as holding pens and *gross motor skills* involving larger movements such as walking and more adventurous active play. These contribute towards muscle development and mobility. Balance and spatial awareness rely on two hidden senses. Firstly, our *proprioceptive sense*, which is to do with our body and spatial awareness and positioning – where, for example, our arm is in relation to other parts of the body. This includes perceiving strength of effort in our muscles and making the necessary adjustments. The other is our *vestibular sense*, which is to do with balance and gravity and helps us to orientate ourselves within the environment and have a sense of movement and balance (Macintyre, 2012). Both senses work alongside other senses such as vision and touch to process external information and are integral for optimal physical development (Goddard-Blythe, 2008). Movement activities such as rocking a child or bringing their hands together to clap, for example, help to exercise the proprioceptive and vestibular systems.

## Sensory perception and sensory integration

Young children learn in multi-sensory ways and a capacity to perceive and process sensory information from all senses is essential for health and well-being. The importance of our ability to process sensory information was highlighted by Ayres (1972) who developed Sensory Integration Theory. Essentially, this theory considers how the body experiences sensations from movement and from the environment, and how the brain structures and organises these sensations so the body can adjust and adapt behaviour accordingly. It is thus a neurological process that enables us to make sense of our world by receiving, registering, modulating, organising and interpreting information that comes to our brains from our senses. If there is a lack of ability to do this effectively then, according to Ayres, this could interfere with the learning and developmental process. Ayres believed that people developed sensory integration through an inherent compulsion to engage in sensorimotor experiences and that this adaptive interaction enabled them to learn from new experiences and challenges. Although aspects of the original theory have been critiqued and modified (Pollock, 2009), the following case study provides an excellent example of sensory integration in practice for a child with behavioural difficulties. One of the key aspects of this example was establishing an enabling environment which allowed the child to feel at ease and contributed to them making progress.

## Case Study

### Sensory integration

Five-year-old James was referred by his school as he had difficulties with motor coordination and concentration which often manifested itself as behavioural difficulties. He was assessed and recommended for sensory integration (SI) therapy. As SI is client-led, the child is allowed to choose their activities, the idea being that they will naturally choose what is good for them. James was very keen to lie down on his tummy (in the hammock) throwing beanbags at large water-filled bottles. He had to organise himself to get in and out of the hammock (motor planning) and needed support with learning how to throw from eye level. He also loved climbing using a rope (pulling against resistance) which stimulated his proprioceptive and vestibular systems. He needed help to begin with but managed on his own after a few sessions. He tried to control everything and needed containment and consistent guidance to help him feel safe and secure. We also worked on balance by hopping on and off rubber jelly pads, and James displayed an amazing imagination for fighting games and escaping from 'the giant crocodile' (a large

*(Continued)*

*(Continued)*

piece of soft play). He loved to swing on the red disc swing which provided further vestibular input. We worked closely together (mum, dad and the occupational therapist) with James and he was happy and engaged in most of the sessions. With this intervention, James made some remarkable progress and felt much more settled in the school situation.

(Linda, occupational therapist, at: http://www.therapy spacebristol.co.uk/)

# Physical play as exercise

If children have space and time to explore their world, they gain spatial awareness and self-awareness as they arrive at an understanding of their bodies, for example, how large they are and whether or not they will fit into a gap beneath a bed during a game of hide and seek; or whether or not they have the strength and the motor skills and coordination to climb certain structures. Physical play, such as ball games, promotes hand-to-eye coordination and develops fitness and health in terms of muscle development and maintaining a healthy body weight. It can increase their mobility, agility and dexterity, alongside cardiovascular fitness such as lung capacity and stamina.

Physical play is of particular importance given that obesity in children has become a serious issue in some Western countries such as the UK. Various programmes have been developed to introduce more physical activity for children, such as the Fundamental Movement Skills (FMS) Programme (Hands et al., 2004). The programme focuses on different aspects of locomotor and body management skills such as balancing, jumping and throwing games and activities. It provides a way of encouraging children's positive attitudes towards movement that will be sustained throughout their lives (Jefferson-Buchanan, 2011). Jefferson-Buchanan stresses the importance of early movement skills in developing cognitive structures in the brain, particularly using repetition of actions to strengthen neural pathways. Moreover, providing the opportunity for movement affords opportunities for young children to engage in social interactions and enables them to develop self-esteem and problem-solving skills. Evidence shows that children who are active go on to continue this active lifestyle in adulthood (Boreham and Riddoch, 2001).

# Outdoor learning

Outdoor learning provides a flexible, dynamic, spatial environment for movement and action which is rich in sensory experiences. Its importance cannot be emphasised enough. Most young children enjoy being outdoors and fresh air and open spaces contribute to their health and well-being in numerous ways, including their sense of freedom and delight (Tovey, 2007). The creation of an enabling environment in an outdoor space provides extensive learning opportunities for personal and social development, physical development, communication, language and literacy, expressive arts and design, mathematics and understanding of the world around them throughout the year (Watts, 2013). Research shows that outdoor play is often more sustained and complex than indoor play (Rogers and Evans, 2006). Provision of outdoor learning environments also addresses concerns of educationalists and child development specialists that children are not connecting with the natural world (Moss, 2012). The following case study provides an example of the learning that can emerge in an outdoor environment and engagement with the natural world.

## Case Study

### Sensory experiences at the seaside

Joycie, who is three, accompanies her mother to the beach. She has had little experience of beaches and sand. At first she tries to run but is unfamiliar with the sinking sensation and loses her balance and falls over. Her mother helps her to her feet and dusts her off saying 'Careful, you need to go more slowly.' Joycie looks intently at the sand and pokes at it with her toes. She wriggles her toes into the warm, fine sand then tentatively takes a step forward. As she gains her balance on the new surface she gains confidence and walks a few more steps but she is still unsure and looks to her mother for reassurance and guidance. Her mother takes her hand and walks further down the beach with her to the high tide line. Here, Joycie encounters seaweed, pebbles and sea debris. She hesitates, then with encouragement from her mother negotiates her way through the tide mark wrinkling her nose in disgust as the unfamiliar textures are uncomfortable beneath her feet. Once past the tide line she experiences a different sensation

*(Continued)*

*(Continued)*

as the sand here is hard and wet. She finds it easier to balance and attempts to run a few steps. As she reaches the sea she again hesitates and explores the wetness with her toes and bends over to touch the sea. A small wave reaches her and she loses her balance and falls over, as it causes the surface beneath her feet to alter with the shifting sands. At this point she becomes distressed as she is wet and it is a shock. She is about to cry, when her mother laughs and says 'Oops-a-daisy – I bet that was that a shock, but isn't this fun?' and scoops her up to a standing position again. She takes the lead from her mother, copies her paddling action and splashes her toes in the water and starts to relax and enjoy the sensation.

There is a wealth of learning evident in the case study. Joycie has learnt about different textures (sand, pebbles, seaweed) and sensations (temperatures and textures of the sand, air and sea, sounds and smells, being unbalanced, falling without being hurt). She has also learnt to trust her mother and has copied her actions in respect of paddling in the sea and understands that this can be a pleasurable activity and 'fun'. She has developed her motor skills and coordination by having the opportunity to adjust her balance on different textured surfaces and by moving between different ground levels as she walked down the beach.

*Forest Schools* provide a particular outdoor learning context and have early years become well-established in many early years settings around the Western world. Forest Schools vary in their mode and application but essentially involve enabling children to experience and explore natural woodland areas (Knight, 2013). Forest Schools support learner-led experiences in natural outdoor spaces throughout all seasons and weathers. For young children, it provides a play-based approach in an environment that is rich in wild, uncultivated areas, offering numerous opportunities to explore, experiment and discover. As with all outdoor learning environments, Forest Schools can encourage children to imagine, create, innovate and manipulate (Forest Schools, 2015). Movement opportunities for balancing and climbing on logs, building and crawling inside dens, collecting sticks and digging holes enable children to use their whole bodies. The physical freedom also provides a vehicle for experiencing and expressing feelings generated by the natural environment. In the next case study, a Forest School trainer narrates stories from a forest school expedition which demonstrates the range of feelings such natural environments inspire, as well as challenging young children to overcome difficulties or make scientific discoveries. It shows how such experiences help to build confidence and self-esteem while developing physical and emotional resilience.

## Case Study

### Forest School in the early years

During a local walk through fields we came to a muddy bank with trees. Some children started to crawl up it on their hands and knees. We tied ropes between the trees at the top and the bottom and showed children how to go up and down using the ropes safely. Some of the more confident children tried this independently. Others wanted adult help for the first few attempts. As they built up their confidence and technique, they became more animated and excited – soon all of the children were using the ropes independent of adult help, laughing and engaging with one another as they climbed and descended.

A child, Rose, asked for a hand jumping off a log, saying she couldn't jump on her own. Some other children followed and jumped off independently. Rose stood and watched as they jumped then went back up and jumped on her own.

A small group of boys thought they found a bone buried under the earth while digging under a bush:

'We found a skeleton!'
'We found a bone!'

They were joined by other children and some of them started excavating around 'the bone' with sticks, investigating and hypothesising about what it could be. We helped to remove it from the ground – 'it's a root of ivy!'

(Julia, Forest School leader and Outdoor Learning practitioner at:
http://www.juliabutlerforestschool.co.uk/)

The importance of such contexts for learning is evident: children are encouraged to be resourceful and take an active part in their own learning experiences; they learn about the natural world and how to assess and take risks. In play spaces and outdoor learning environments, where decisions have been made to satisfy health and safety regulations, the health benefits of play may be overridden by attempts to reduce potential injury.

However, we need to strike a *risk/benefit* balance between keeping young children safe and enabling them to take risks. If we tip this balance too much by creating a risk-free environment we may be impeding children's health and well-being by denying them the opportunity to develop skills and coping strategies that will lead them to make accurate risk assessments and build their capacity to avoid real danger (Spiegal et al., 2014).

## Mindful Moment

Think back to your own childhood experiences of playing outdoors. What do you remember most? How did it feel? What learning occurred?

# Physical play and cognitive development

The repetitive and explorative movements afforded by physical play not only stimulate the motor regions of the brain, they also provide extensive opportunities for developing other parts of the brain, such as interpreting and understanding the environment, categorising and sequencing, reasoning and problem-solving and using the imagination. Children learn through actively *experiencing* and actively *experimenting*, and this develops their *cognitive* abilities. Invariably this occurs by accident at first (such as when an infant knocks a dangling toy with their hand) which leads on to a trial and error process. For example, an infant, who has learned to access toys from a box where you lift the lid might be perplexed when presented with a box that does not open in this way. By trial and error, and a motivation to access the toys within the box, they discover that the lid slides open. This requires a different action and a revision of the motor skill involved.

According to Piagetian theory, the new box caused a state of *cognitive disequilibrium*, which the child finds uncomfortable and even distressing (Berger, 2011). By a process of mental adjustment and *adaptation* to the new experience children *assimilate* the experience but may have to *accommodate* it – in other words change their existing understanding or mental representation ('schema') about how boxes open. By changing an existing schema or pattern of thought and actions about how boxes open, they arrive at a state of *equilibrium* (or mental balance). The restoration of mental balance helps the child to calm down and in the process they have learnt a new skill. This experience becomes stored in their memory through repetition, so when faced with a similar situation they can retrieve this information and apply it as part of their problem-solving capability. Wood (2011) makes the point that children play a role in constructing their own knowledge and use their previous experiences in order to make sense of their current situation.

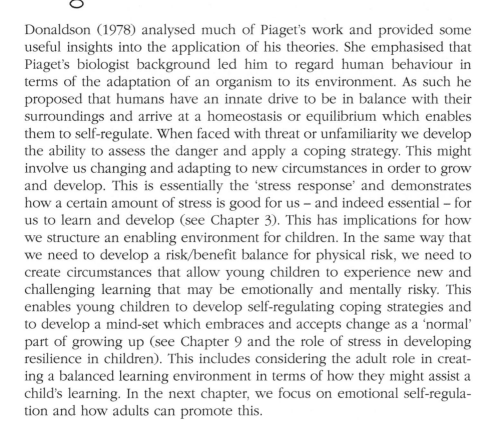

### Mindful Moment

Can you describe an observation of a young child who is experiencing a new toy or object? What was their reaction? What did they learn from experimentation with the toy or object? Does Piaget's *theory of equilibration* fit with the pattern of behaviour that you observed?

Donaldson (1978) analysed much of Piaget's work and provided some useful insights into the application of his theories. She emphasised that Piaget's biologist background led him to regard human behaviour in terms of the adaptation of an organism to its environment. As such he proposed that humans have an innate drive to be in balance with their surroundings and arrive at a homeostasis or equilibrium which enables them to self-regulate. When faced with threat or unfamiliarity we develop the ability to assess the danger and apply a coping strategy. This might involve us changing and adapting to new circumstances in order to grow and develop. This is essentially the 'stress response' and demonstrates how a certain amount of stress is good for us – and indeed essential – for us to learn and develop (see Chapter 3). This has implications for how we structure an enabling environment for children. In the same way that we need to develop a risk/benefit balance for physical risk, we need to create circumstances that allow young children to experience new and challenging learning that may be emotionally and mentally risky. This enables young children to develop self-regulating coping strategies and to develop a mind-set which embraces and accepts change as a 'normal' part of growing up (see Chapter 9 and the role of stress in developing resilience in children). This includes considering the adult role in creating a balanced learning environment in terms of how they might assist a child's learning. In the next chapter, we focus on emotional self-regulation and how adults can promote this.

## Key Points

- Active learning has two strands: the child taking an active role in their own learning and the physiological dimensions of active learning and development.
- Active learning provides integration of brain, mind and body development.
- Learning through play provides an important medium for physical health and well-being.
- Physical play promotes psychomotor and cognitive development facilitated by providing balanced, enabling environments in early years settings extending into the natural world.

# Useful Further Reading and Websites

- Goddard-Blythe, S. (2008) *What Babies and Children Really Need*. Stroud: Hawthorne Press. This provides an excellent overview of children's sensory and physical development, highlighting their importance for health and well-being.
- Moylett, H. (2013) 'How young children learn: introduction and overview', in H. Moylett (ed.), *Characteristics of Effective Early Learning*. Maidenhead: Open University Press. This is a valuable review of the characteristics of effective learning and synthesises key research and pedagogy related to play and active learning.
- The Institute of Neuro-Physiological Psychology is a valuable source of information regarding neuro-physiological development at: http://www.inpp.org.uk/.
- Early Education has guidelines for developmental milestones at: https://www.early-education.org.uk.

# CHAPTER 8

# EMOTION COACHING

---

## Chapter Overview

This chapter turns its attention to a particular strategy that can help to create an optimal, enabling environment for emotional well-being. It does so by outlining the key tenets and processes of a strategy called Emotion Coaching. Emotion Coaching helps to generate nurturing relationships that scaffold the development of effective stress management skills in order to promote emotional and behavioural self-regulation. This evidence-based approach provides practitioners with a valuable tool for supporting children's behaviour and harnesses well-being for both adults and children. It draws on recent research conducted by Rose and Gilbert.

---

## A relational model of behaviour management

Common behaviour management strategies include the use of reward stickers and charts and time-out as a means of teaching young children how to behave. Although this might not be something you use in your practice, most behaviour management techniques in early years settings often rely on traditional, behaviourist approaches for modifying young children's behaviour. Behaviourism is based on the premise that behaviour can be controlled and modified via the reinforcement systems of rewards and/or sanctions. It dates notably to the work of Skinner (1974). Despite its critics and considerable psychological advances in the understanding of children's motivation in relation to self-concept, self-esteem and self-regulation (Gerhardt, 2004; Lawrence, 2006), behaviourist principles are still evident in many behaviour policies in settings, with rewards and sanctions used as key tools for controlling young children's behaviour (Ellis and Tod, 2009).

The behaviourist approach has been criticised for relying on *external* frameworks for moderating behaviour and ignoring the feelings which underlie the behaviour (Gottman et al., 1997). Although it can be a powerful way of conditioning children to behave, it means that children largely learn to rely on rewards or live in fear of punishment to make them behave. Once the reward or fear has been removed, such children may not be able to self-regulate their behaviour. Research has also shown that children soon habituate to reward systems and so they begin to lose their effectiveness to motivate children to behave (Ellis and Tod, 2009). Similarly, too much fear can lead to children relying on innate survival mechanisms such as disassociation (i.e. not caring) or becoming reactive (i.e. aggressive) in an attempt to compensate for the fear of punishment (Cairns, 2001). It is also apparent that rewards and sanctions just do not work for all children, particularly children with additional needs. This is often because a behaviourist approach relies not only on children's capacity to mentally envisage and understand the consequences of their behaviour, but also on an ability to delay gratification or regulate innate emotional needs and these abilities may not be possible for some children. There are also the particularly vulnerable children whose priority to feel safe and secure overwhelms any capacity to respond to a behaviour management system that relies on a fully functioning rational mind (Cairns, 2001).

This chapter draws attention to a growing base of research evidence which suggests that a *relational* rather than a behavioural approach to supporting young children's learning and behaviour is likely to facilitate the development of better self-regulation and social functioning (Shaughnessy, 2012). Such an approach operates to create *internal* mechanisms within the brain rather than relying on external controls. An approach that encapsulates this more *affective* and effective way of managing behaviour is called Emotion Coaching. It reflects the evidence that the most successful programmes, in terms of improving behaviour for learning, are those that focus on the *emotional* and *social causes* of difficult to manage behaviour and proactively teach social and emotional competencies (Weare and Gray, 2003). For example, it recognises that socially competent children who are able to regulate their emotions are better equipped in terms of school readiness and go on to achieve higher academic success than those who lack impulse control or have poor social skills (Webster-Stratton and Reid, 2004). Emotion Coaching is also supported by recent findings from neuroscience (Gottman et al., 1997).

## Mindful Moment

Think about the behaviour support system in your setting or in a setting you have experienced – what features of practice reflect a relational or behavioural model of behaviour management?

# What is Emotion Coaching?

Emotion Coaching is based on the work of John Gottman and his colleagues in America who emphasise the process of *emotional regulation* rather than behaviour modification – in other words, a focus on the *feelings* and *desires* which are ultimately driving the behaviour instead of just the behaviour itself. As Gottman writes: 'Emotion coaching is about helping children to understand the different emotions they experience, why they occur, and how to handle them' (Gottman and DeClaire, 1997: 2). In England, personal, social and emotional development is a primary responsibility for professionals working with young children (DfE, 2014a). Emotion Coaching can enable practitioners to take advantage of opportune moments to teach appropriate behaviour *in the moment that it occurs*. An Emotion Coaching approach also reflects the capacity to be both aware of our *own* as well as children's emotions. Adults who are *mind-minded*, i.e. who tune into young children's thoughts and feelings, help to scaffold children's understanding of their own behaviour. Gottman et al.'s (1997) research has shown that emotion coached children:

- achieve more academically in school;
- are more popular;
- have fewer behavioural problems;
- have fewer infectious illnesses;
- are more emotionally stable;
- are more resilient.

Emotion Coaching views all behaviour as a *form of communication* and makes an important distinction between children's behaviour and the feelings that *underlie* that behaviour. A key belief is that all emotions are acceptable, but not all behaviour. It is about helping children to understand their different emotions as they experience them, why they occur and how to handle them, leading to happier, more resilient and well-adjusted children. It is essentially comprised of two key elements – *empathy* and *guidance*. These two elements underpin the adults' approach whenever *emotional moments* occur. Emotional empathy involves recognising, labelling and validating a child's emotions, regardless of the behaviour, in order to promote self-awareness of emotions. The circumstances might also require setting limits on appropriate behaviour (such as stating clearly what is acceptable behaviour) and possible consequential action (such as implementing behaviour management procedures). However, key to this process is guidance: engagement with the child in problem-solving in order to support children's ability to learn to self-regulate and to seek alternative courses of action preventing future transgressions – but only when their brains are in a *receptive* state for such problem-solving.

Gottman has described Emotion Coaching as involving five steps:

1. Be aware of the child's responses.
2. Recognise emotional times as opportunities for intimacy and teaching.
3. Listen empathetically and validate the child's feelings.
4. Help the child to verbally label emotions – helps soothe the nervous system and recovery rate.
5. Set limits while helping the child to problem-solve.

Research by Rose and Gilbert has shown that these five steps can be perceived more simply in three steps for the busy practitioner (Rose et al., 2015; Gilbert et al., 2014):

STEP 1 – Recognising, empathising, validating and labelling feelings

STEP 2 – Limit setting

STEP 3 – Problem-solving

## How do we do Emotion Coaching?

The first of the steps of Emotion Coaching is *essential* and often the step that is forgotten when dealing with children's behaviour. Frequently, practitioners rely on reason to distract or dissuade a child. However, when a child is in an emotional state, particularly if it is intense, they are unable to engage with the more rational parts of their brain (the frontal lobes) since their mind and body is locked in a flight/flight state. You may recall from earlier chapters how neuroscientific research has shown sensory information (visual, auditory, olfactory) is sent first to the limbic system *before* being processed in the decision-making areas of the brain (the frontal lobes). If the sensory information is deemed to be a real or imagined threat, the limbic system signals the rest of the body to mobilise into a fight/flight response. Remember that a 'threat' might simply be the result of a normal and thwarted desire, such as not wanting to share a toy.

Children in an emotional state need to be returned to a relaxed, calm state before we can reason with them. Gottman and DeClaire (1997) believe that if we propose solutions before we empathise, it is the equivalent to trying to build a house before any firm foundation has been laid. What children need when they are angry or sad, no matter how badly they might be behaving, is *emotional first aid*. Since feelings are self-justifying, a practitioner needs to get *in sync* with a child by recognising and then affirming the existence of their feelings. Empathy from the practitioner helps the child to calm down, providing a safe haven of acceptance that builds emotional and responsive bonds between the practitioner and child. Once the child has calmed, she/he is more open and able to reason and the practitioner can work with the child in creating effective neural connections to the rational parts of the brain (the frontal lobes) to become an efficient manager of emotion (Goleman,1995).

# Disapproving and dismissing styles of behaviour management

Gottman has also drawn attention to the less effective ways of supporting children's behaviour. This research shows that adopting what is known as a *disapproving* style or a *dismissing* style does not help the child to learn to self-regulate or develop resilience (Gottman et al., 1997). A disapproving approach to behaviour management views emotions as a sign of weakness or lack of control. A disapproving adult lacks empathy and may be noticeably critical and intolerant and try to get rid of negative emotions via discipline, reprimand or punishment. A disapproving practitioner focuses on the behaviour of the child rather than the emotions generating the behaviour. In this kind of response, emotional displays are viewed as a form of manipulation, a lack of obedience or a sign of bad character. Behaviour management strategies are motivated by a need to control or regain power and/or to toughen up the child and are commonly expressed through a stern and angry tone. Although it may appear successful in the short term, a disapproving style is probably the least effective way of developing more long-term, positive behaviour in a child, particularly because the adult is role modelling an angry response.

Similarly, a dismissing style of behaviour management views children's emotional displays as toxic. Emotions such as anger need to be got over quickly. This kind of adult considers that paying attention to such emotions will make them worse and prolong the emotional state. Therefore, a dismissing adult will try to stop emotions by minimising or making light of their importance – by dismissing them. It is important to distinguish a dismissing style from a disapproving style as it can often appear to be a warmer and more empathic response. Indeed, it is often motivated by a desire to rescue and make things better for the child. However, it relies on logic and/or distraction/reward to try and help the child feel better. Common phrases might be 'Don't worry about it', 'Be a big girl' or 'You'll be fine'.

Although a dismissing style is gentler and less dictatorial than the disapproving way of managing children's behaviour, it does not allow the child to engage with how they are *feeling*. Distraction or disapproval approaches can often work and temporarily stop unacceptable behaviour – but they deliver a message to the children that what they are feeling is not right, that their assessment is wrong and that they should not feel this way. They are not able to learn to distinguish between *feeling* and *behaviour*. Children experiencing disapproving or dismissing styles of interaction do not learn to trust what they are feeling. Such styles of interaction also tend to lead to the suppression of innate and natural emotions or to a reliance on distraction/reward to reduce the intensity of the feeling, since they are not given opportunities to *experience* them (and this may generate more negative emotions such as shame and resentment). A lack of experience and understanding of an emotional state can, in turn, affect children's capacity to manage feelings by themselves or to employ *self-regulation* to reduce the intensity of the emotions. A reduced capacity to self-soothe affects their ability to engage the more rational parts of their brain and to make appropriate behavioural decisions or to develop problem-solving strategies to resolve the situation.

## Mindful Moment

Gottman's differentiation of adults responding to a child's emotional state (disapproving, dismissing, emotion coaching) led him to create the term *meta-emotion philosophy*. This refers to the thoughts and feelings an individual has about their own emotions and those of others, which

> in turn affects how they respond to and deal with their own and other people's emotions (Gottman et al., 1997). This correlates with reflective functioning and emotional intelligence discussed in Chapter 5.
>
> Consider your own responses to challenging behaviour and how they affect your emotional well-being.
>
> Can you envisage how Emotion Coaching might assist you in your own capacity to self-regulate your emotional responses?

# Role modelling empathy

The issue of adults role modelling appropriate emotional responses becomes particularly significant when we consider mirror neurons. These specialised brain cells were discussed in an earlier chapter and you will recall that they are activated simply by watching or copying intentional actions. Thus mirror neurons literally enable us to mirror the behaviour of others. In relation to behaviour management, some neuroscientists consider that the mirror neuron system provides the building blocks for empathy and socialisation by building our capacity to emulate others and understanding others' intent (Le Page and Theoret, 2007). Simply put, if we are trying to support a child who has pushed another child and we respond with a cross face, a pointing finger and an angry tone, the mirror neurons in the child's brain are likely to be trying to emulate the same response. This is probably the opposite of what we wish to convey in the already angry child. Instead, we ought to be role modelling a more empathic response to the child's emotional state in order to foster a more empathic way of behaving that will help the child to inhibit their desire to push another child and develop more pro-social ways of engaging with others.

A common concern regarding the practice of Emotion Coaching is the fear that empathising with children during instances of misbehaviour might give the appearance of endorsing the negative behaviour. In our research, we were often asked: 'Will all that empathising just mean children will think it is OK to behave badly?' Another fear is that practitioners might feel weak and less in control if they empathise with the child (Rose et al., 2015). However, it is important to remember that Emotion Coaching also involves establishing the boundaries of acceptable behaviour and *limit-setting*. You can condone the *feeling* underlying the behaviour, but not the behaviour itself.

The messages children receive when they experience an Emotion Coaching style is that we all have feelings, that they are all natural and normal, and that they create wishes and desires which are normal too, but that feelings may need to be regulated and expressed constructively and that such wishes and desires may not be met. It conveys to the child that they are not alone, that they are accepted, supported, valid, cared about, understood, trusted and respected. At the same time, it communicates that not all behaviours are acceptable, that they cannot always get what they want and that they might need to moderate how to express feelings and desires. In other words, an Emotion Coaching approach acknowledges that all desires, wishes and feelings are acceptable but that their fulfilment or expression of them might not be. This supports children's learning in how to resolve their issues and empowers them to feel safe enough to engage in their own problem-solving. Thus through Emotion Coaching a child learns to empathise, to read others' emotions and social cues, to control impulses, self-soothe and self-regulate, to delay gratification, to motivate themselves and to cope with life's ups and downs (be resilient) (Gottman et al., 1997). It also shows children how conflicts might be resolved peacefully through self-control, and builds problem solving capacity and well-being.

## Self-regulation through co-regulation

Emotion Coaching offers a powerful way to connect with young children's emotional state and helps them to manage their own feelings and desires – they learn to *self-regulate* their behaviour internally rather than relying on extrinsic rewards or sanctions to modify their behaviour.

A key process involved in Emotion Coaching is *co-regulation*. By empathising with a child's emotional state, even when they are displaying inappropriate behaviour, we are providing a support structure for that child to learn to self-regulate. We do this for all other aspects of their learning. For example, we help children learn to talk by talking to them – this narrative helps children to engage and respond and begin to articulate their own words. With Emotion Coaching, we are providing a similar scaffold and narrative for them to learn about their own emotions and how they can be regulated. Once again, we can turn to some recent neuroscientific evidence to help us understand how important co-regulation is in helping children to self-regulate and to develop good vagal tone (Gottman et al., 1997). You may recall from the early chapters how vagal tone plays an important part in helping us to regulate stress. Gottman's research shows that Emotion Coaching appears to have an effective impact on the operation of the vagus nerve since the techniques of Emotion Coaching can trigger the vagus nerve into helping the brain and body to calm down, enabling the child to develop better vagal tone. While young children's brains and nervous systems are still under construction, it is of particular importance for the early years practitioner to help support children in developing their vagal tone. Gottman and DeClaire provide a useful metaphor to explain this – they comment that just as children with good muscle tone do well in sporting activities, children who have good vagal tone are better at responding to and recovering from emotional stress (1997).

The first few chapters also revealed the importance of integration within different parts of the brain and body in order to develop well-being. Emotion Coaching is particularly effective, not only in soothing the limbic system, but also in enabling practitioners to help children to connect the limbic system to the frontal lobes and to process experiences in an integrated way. It also helps to create a context for stimulating both the left and right hemispheres of the brain, linking empathy with rational thinking simultaneously.

## Internal 'dialogues'

Havighurst et al. (2009) have highlighted how Emotion Coaching can contribute to children's Internal Working Models. In Chapter 5, we explored how Internal Working Models are created and how they guide children's thoughts, feelings and behaviour. Attachment research has shown how *emotion-focused talk* by the adult can teach children to use appropriate strategies to cope with stress, literally helping to build the architecture of their brains (Schore, 1994). This links to the idea of reflective functioning discussed in Chapter 6 as well as to the work of Vygotsky (1978) and his notion of an internal dialogue. Emotion Coaching assists the child to develop an internal dialogue about social and emotional experiences and aids them in regulating their emotions and social behaviour. It is essentially a dialogic process which enables children to feel appreciated, to explore their feelings and relationships, to reflect with others and to confront their anger, fear and anxiety, rather than projecting them through challenging behaviour (Matthews, 2006).

When a practitioner talks to a child about their emotional state and then supports them to moderate their responses and develop strategies for more pro-social behaviour, a child will develop a capacity to 'think about feelings', to 'take an interest in the mental states of others', and 'shape the pattern of the way [s/he] responds to the situations in which [they] find

[them]selves' (Haddon et al., 2005: 6). Drawing on the work of Damasio, Haddon et al. (2005) discuss how the linkages between the affective and cognitive areas of the brain shape our capacity to assess situations and make effective decisions as well as form positive relationships and have a sense of self-efficacy.

In essence, Emotion Coaching provides the practitioner with an effective strategy which helps children learn to self-regulate their emotions and consequently their behaviour:

- by triggering a calmer response through empathetic support;
- by assisting/co-regulating young children to self-soothe in raising their awareness of their own emotional state and helping them to establish better vagal tone;
- by using the emotional moment as an opportunity to scaffold young children's self-management of their emotions and behaviour.

## Does it work in practice?

Recent research in England has evaluated the impact of adopting Emotion Coaching techniques into professional practice, particularly during behavioural incidents (Rose et al., 2015; Gilbert et al., 2014). Practitioners and parents were trained and supported to help embed Emotion Coaching into practice and preliminary findings show that Emotion Coaching:

- helps children to regulate, improve and take ownership of their behaviour;
- helps children to calm down and better understand their emotions;
- helps practitioners to be more sensitive to children's needs;
- helps create more consistent responses to children's behaviour;
- helps practitioners to feel more 'in control' during incidents;
- helps promote positive relationships.

For example, one practitioner talked about how Emotion Coaching helped her to communicate more effectively and consistently with children in stressful situations and to de-escalate volatile situations. She said: 'It made the whole situation feel less fraught for both parties.' By using Emotion Coaching, adults found difficult situations less stressful and exhausting with a positive impact not just on the children's well-being, but on their own. One said: 'It actually made me feel better because it made me feel calmer during the process.' Another said: 'I show more empathy with how the child must be feeling and it helps you slow down to consider why a child is upset/angry. Because I now use this, I think the relationship I have with the children is much more relaxed.'

Emotion Coaching promotes young children's self-awareness of their emotions and positive self-regulation of their behaviour, and generates more nurturing relationships. In nurturing relationships, young children can feel protected, comforted and secure within a context of caring and trustworthy adults, who can support them in their emotional self-regulation. As one practitioner put it: 'It makes the children feel more secure and gives them a vocabulary to talk about how they are feeling instead of just acting out. This helps them to be more positive and happier.' Meanwhile a parent commented: 'My boys seem to calm down a lot quicker than before and my daughter is understanding that she's not on her own with her emotions. Their confidence is improving and they know it's normal to have all these feelings.'

By using an example from the research project where Emotion Coaching was used successfully in a nursery, we can see how it might work in practice.

## Case Study

### Emotion Coaching at nursery

Sam was a two-and-a-half-year-old who was looked after mostly by his grandmother as his mother had health issues. He had not spent much time in the nursery and when the time came for his grandmother to leave him, he would become very upset, often screaming for a long time. At first the Key Person would try and entice him to stop crying by saying 'If you stop crying, I'll give you a cuddle' or 'If you stop crying, I'll give you your teddy', or she put him in the time-out chair on his own until he eventually stopped crying. These attempts to reward and/or distract Sam into behaving differently did not seem to be helping. After Emotion Coaching training, the Key Person changed the way she approached Sam in the following way.

When she next saw Sam, she immediately started to focus on Sam's emotional state, empathising with how he might be feeling and affirming these feelings by verbalising them for him by saying: 'Ah, I can see you're sad Sam. It's making you feel upset to leave your Grandma. I can understand why you feel like that. This is a new place for you, isn't it? That would feel strange for me too.' In this way, she was co-regulating

*(Continued)*

*(Continued)*

his emotional state (rather than leaving him to cope on his own) by tuning into his feelings. She was also role modelling a more empathic response and providing a narrative for Sam to help trigger a calmer state and engage in more productive behaviour. After he was soothed, she would make it clear that screaming was not OK but would go through some ideas of what he could do instead when he was feeling upset. She would say: 'There are things we can do to make you feel better when you come to nursery; things that will help you not to cry so hard and make such a noise. Let's find a special place you can go when you come to nursery and we can sit together until you feel better.' The Key Person noticed that using Step 1 of Emotion Coaching helped Sam to calm down more quickly, that using Step 2 helped Sam to learn some of the boundaries of acceptable behaviour and that Step 3 helped her to work with Sam to find strategies that would help him to settle more easily into nursery. Although the Key Person used some distraction techniques which might be viewed as a reward to motivate Sam, this was done within the internal Emotion Coaching framework which helped Sam to moderate his feelings and behaviour, rather than just rely on external rewards.

Emotion Coaching is for all children but has also successfully supported children with additional needs. For example, it has been used effectively with children who have conduct disorders and those exposed to violent environments, including inter-parental violence, maltreatment and community violence. Emotion Coaching has also been positively correlated with secure attachments and improved the psychological functioning of children who have complex needs (see Gus et al., 2015). Overall, Emotion Coaching instils the tools that will aid children's ability to self-regulate their emotions and behaviour (Gus et al., 2015). Table 8.1 summarises the main aspects of the Emotion Coaching process.

The implications of early behavioural difficulties and their association with mental health problems, crime, substance abuse and relationship and parenthood difficulties highlight the importance of utilising effective strategies to help compensate for early difficulties (DfE, 2011). Of course Emotion Coaching is not a panacea, a quick fix or a miracle cure. Gopnik et al. (1999) talk about how expressing emotions appropriately and using this learning to maintain relationships can be one of the most complex challenges we have to learn. This becomes even more difficult

**Table 8.1**   Emotion Coaching

---

*Key points to remember for Step 1:*

- Recognise all emotions as being natural and normal and not always a matter of choice
- Recognise behaviour as communication (relational vs behavioural model)
- Look for physical and verbal signs of the emotion being felt
- Take on the child's perspective (mentalising/mind-mindedness)
- Use words to reflect back child's emotion and help child/young person to label emotion
- Affirm and empathise, allowing to calm down
- Provide a narrative/translation for the emotional experience (creating cognitive links)

*Key points to remember for Step 2:*

- State the boundary limits of acceptable behaviour
- Make it clear certain behaviours cannot be accepted
- But retain the child's self-dignity (crucial for responsive behaviour and well-being)

*Key points to remember for Step 3:*

When the child is calm and in a relaxed, rational state:

- Explore the feelings that give rise to the behaviour/problem/incident
- Scaffold alternative ideas and actions that could lead to more appropriate and productive outcomes
- Empower the child to believe s/he can overcome difficulties and manage feelings/behaviour

---

when differing cultural expectations and codes of conduct create potential conflict for young children. But engagement in Emotion Coaching can provide transferable skills that benefit practitioners, parents and children. In this respect, it contributes to sustainable early years practice that optimises universal well-being and resilience.

## Mindful Moment

Now that you have an insight into Emotion Coaching as a strategy for supporting children's behaviour and well-being, how might it be implemented into your own working practice?

What could be the challenges for you in using Emotion Coaching in your setting?

## Key Points

- Emotion Coaching promotes emotional and behavioural self-regulation by helping to process feelings through co-regulating intense emotions and providing a narrative of the experience.
- It involves recognising, empathising, validating and labelling emotions, then setting limits (if needed) and finally engaging in problem-solving solutions when the child is in a calm state.
- It operates within a nurturing relationship and scaffolds the development of effective stress management skills.
- It provides a relational model of behavioural support for early years practitioners.

## Useful Further Reading and Websites

- Gottman, J. and DeClaire, J. (1997) *The Heart of Parenting: How to Raise an Emotionally Intelligent Child*. New York: Fireside. An easy-to-read summary of Gottman's work on Emotion Coaching.
- Gilbert, L., Rose, J. and McGuire-Snieckus, R. (2014) 'Promoting children's well-being and sustainable citizenship through emotion coaching', in M. Thomas (ed.), *A Child's World: Working Together for a Better Future*. Aberystwyth: Aberystwyth Press. A helpful insight into some of the research on Emotion Coaching and how it translates into practice.
- The Emotion Coaching UK website provides information on Emotion Coaching and training routes in the UK at: http://emotioncoachinguk.com
- The Gottman Institute in the USA provides access to resources on Emotion Coaching at: http://emotioncoaching.gottman.com/.

# CHAPTER 9

# RESILIENCE AND BUILDING LEARNING POWER

## Chapter Overview

This chapter considers young children's resilience and learning. It highlights how early years practitioners can encourage children to believe in their own abilities so that they are able to succeed in tasks, attain goals and experience a sense of achievement and how this can help to raise their self-esteem and improve their health and well-being. It begins by exploring the ideas surrounding the development of resilience and *self-efficacy* in children. It focuses, in particular, on how these issues affect learning and Building Learning Power. It will show how Learning Power is an enabling factor in the development of young children and their health and well-being. Key learning skills, considered to be integral to effective learning, will be examined and how the combination of *feeling*, *thinking* and *doing* forms the basis for health and well-being.

## Resilience

Resilience relates to our capacity to pick ourselves up, learn from our mistakes and perhaps tackle tasks with increased vigour and determination to succeed, or develop alternative strategies to move forward.

Resilience is intricately linked to our capacity to process, manage and overcome stress and trauma. It is a universal capacity that can enable a person to prevent, minimise or overcome the damaging effect of adversity (Grotberg, 1995). It is important to recognise that resilience is not a trait or a characteristic. Is a complex *process* involving both internal cognitive and personality factors *and* the functioning of external *protective* factors, such as caring adults, so we would not label children as *resilient* or *not resilient* but rather think in terms of children who are *manifesting resilient behaviours* and those who are not. From a neurological perspective, resilience is evident within our brains. For example, people identified as having resilience have greater activity in the frontal lobes. Resilient brains have up to 30 times more activity in the frontal lobes than non-resilient brains and more neural connections between the lower and upper regions of the brain (Music, 2011). These neural connections play an important role in facilitating recovery from adversity. These connections are forged by our early relationships and experiences.

Grotberg's (1995) international research has identified three key sources which help to create a resilient child. These are social and interpersonal supports, personal, inner strengths and interpersonal and problem-solving skills. These features are listed in Table 9.1.

**Table 9.1**   Features of a resilient child

---

**I HAVE (social and interpersonal supports)**

- People around me I trust and who love me, no matter what
- People who set limits for me so I know when to stop before there is danger or trouble
- People who show me how to do things right by the way they do things
- People who want me to learn to do things on my own
- People who help me when I am sick, in danger or need to learn

**I AM (personal, inner strengths)**

- A person people can like and love
- Glad to do nice things for others and show my concern
- Respectful of myself and others
- Willing to be responsible for what I do
- Sure things will be all right

**I CAN (interpersonal problem-solving skills)**

- Talk to others about things that frighten me or bother me
- Find ways to solve problems that I face
- Control myself when I feel like doing something not right or dangerous
- Figure out when it is a good time to talk to someone or to take action
- Find someone to help me when I need it

(Grotberg, 1995)

---

**Mindful Moment**

Think about your own resources of resilience – compile your own **I have,
I am** and **I can** chart.

Now think about what you can do as an early years practitioner
that can promote the support, strengths and skills needed to promote
resilience.

Another model that considered the attributes needed for resilience and
relates these to children's learning is encapsulated in Claxton's (2002)
notion of Building Learning Power.

# Building Learning Power

For Claxton (1999, 2002), resilience is one of four factors that enhance
children's Learning Power. He considers how children's Learning Power
can be enhanced by focusing on areas that he has identified as being
fundamental to the development of their learning capacity: resilience,
resourcefulness, reciprocity and reflection. These four areas are known
as the four R's and will be considered in detail.

## Resilience

Resilience has already been discussed and defined to some extent. It is the
ability to harness a determination to find a way of coping with, or managing, a situation. However, it does not mean you will never experience
feeling overwhelmed by the task ahead of you or by a situation you find
stressful (Cottrell, 2013). Claxton's (2002) view of resilience emphasises the
ability to focus and concentrate on the current task so that external influences do not distract you from making progress. This single-mindedness of
purpose leads to tenacity and perseverance to acquire skills or to grasp
ideas which support the development of capabilities and understanding.

## Resourcefulness

Resourcefulness is the ability to develop different strategies and draw upon
one's own resources when coping with a situation that requires a different

approach in order to achieve one's goals. Many of us do not recognise how resourceful we are until faced with a situation that pushes us out of our comfort zone. Such a situation might cause an element of stress and even anxiety, but this is where a certain amount of tolerable stress enables us to develop different strategies and draw upon resources that we did not know we were capable of accessing. Stress can mobilise us to action. If we are able to regulate the stress and reduce the anxiety, we can reflect upon the experience (see 'Reflection' below) and consider our achievements. As a result we can derive an enhanced sense of self-esteem and a better understanding of our self-efficacy, which in turn leads to an increased self-awareness, which has an impact upon our health and well-being.

## Reciprocity/relationships

Reciprocity is about the relationships in learning. Claxton (2002) considers how learning situations involve *orchestrating, explaining* and *commentating* by practitioners and how learning experiences are *modelled* on others. Learning cannot take place in a vacuum and invariably relies upon other people to inform and create our learning experiences. For example, in a group learning situation, such as a problem-solving task, the goal of the exercise might appear to be to solve the problem, but incidental learning may also occur, such as learning about ourselves as a learner within a group – whether we took a lead, whether we learnt by observing, whether we collated others' ideas or facilitated others' learning. In assisting others and explaining processes we also learn about our own learning.

## Reflection

For meaningful learning to take place there needs to be reflection on what we have learnt and also *how* we have learnt – in other words, the *process* of learning – as this can inform future learning. Reflection might not be immediate but may require time and distance so that our minds can process how we approached the task, the difficulties we encountered, how we felt about doing the task and – the important part – how we would change our approach if we replicated the task. It is from this reflection and acknowledgement of our strengths and limitations that the greatest learning can occur. This includes reflecting on when we make mistakes or do not achieve a goal. It is important to evaluate our actions in a positive light. If we do not learn to develop a capacity to learn from our mistakes, we may personalise this as a failure, which may affect our self-esteem and resilience to continue learning. This can be detrimental and impede progress if we transmute failure in one situation to another, forming a future barrier to learning.

## Mindful Moment

Think of a learning task that you found challenging. Can you relate your experience to the four R's:

- *Resilience*. Did you display resilience in tackling the task? Did you achieve your goal?
- *Reciprocity*. Who helped or encouraged you and how did they do this?
- *Resourcefulness*. What resources did you draw upon to cope with the situation?
- *Reflection*. Reflect upon the process and/or the task – what did you learn about your own learning?

# The relationship between the four R's

There is a clear overlap between the four facets of learning and they are interconnected. Relationships interact with reflective processes which can help a child to identify their own resourcefulness and in turn can assist them in the process of harnessing their resilience and determination to succeed in future tasks. The following case study from a Wiltshire primary school provides an example of Building Learning Power in practice and how it might be applied in an early years classroom.

## Case Study

### Building Learning Power in practice

At Fynamore Primary School, Wiltshire, Building Learning Power (BLP) was introduced to the Reception children through stories that brought the complex words of Resilience, Resourcefulness, Reciprocity and Reflection to life. For example, rather than considering the term Reciprocity in isolation, the children announced themselves as Reciprocal Rabbits that worked as a team, while they conducted tasks such as carrying boxes together across the classroom.

Each of the four R's was represented by a particular creature which stood for the BLP aspect and as such this enabled a common language that could be used and understood by both pupils and early years practitioners.

*(Continued)*

*(Continued)*

Wall charts were used to display the four R's and to identify which R they were using or achieving. Each of the four R's has acted as a powerful motivator in encouraging independence and building self-esteem. For example, one child in the class who had difficulties with hand–eye coordination and scissor control chose the most challenging shape to cut out. However, the challenge did not deter her and she worked for a sustained period of 20 minutes. This determination and perseverance was praised and encouraged by the adult. The child declared, 'I'm being a Resilient Robin, because I'm not giving up!' The model gave the children an opportunity for reflection, validated the child's effort and sharing the accomplishment with others, such as visitors to the classroom, boosted the child's self-esteem. Equally, resilience has been used to challenge and encourage children working at the highest level within the class. For these children, an understanding of resilience has provided validation that the journey is just as important, if not more so, than the final outcome. They have been able to demonstrate tenacity and perseverance which has allowed them to overcome fear of failure and grow and develop. For some of the most able children, this common language has begun to provide a sense of relief as they previously may have been worried about failing.

(Rosie Pritchard, teacher, Fynamore School)

**Figure 9.1**   BLP display of animal symbolisation for Learning Power

(Display by Tracey Barnett, teacher, Fynamore School)

# Adult assistance – the skilled practitioner

As we have seen, the development of resilience is predicated on inter-personal relationships. This resonates with the work of Vygotsky and his theory of the Zone of Proximal Development (ZPD). Vygotsky's (1978) theory represented a social constructivist view that stressed the importance of the social context of learning. He recognised that there are tasks a child can complete independently and tasks which are too difficult for them to manage alone; somewhere in between is the Zone of Proximal Development. Berger (2011) refers to this as the *magic middle*, where the child can achieve a task through the assistance of more knowledgeable others. 'Tasks at this level would be stimulating, challenging and attainable with assistance' (Richards, 2011a: 43).

An enabling environment needs to promote a balance between offering children opportunities to reinforce learning and to stimulate new learning. If the new learning challenge seems insurmountable and does not fit with the child's *perception* of what is achievable, then the child may disengage and it may be difficult to persuade them to attempt the task, so practitioners may be able to work within the child's ZPD to support their progression. If the learning is broken into smaller, manageable steps, then the task is less onerous and may feel attainable – it provides a *scaffold* for the child, to coin Bruner's term (Wood et al., 1976). The role of the adult might entail encouragement or lending a helping hand when the energy and enthusiasm appears to flag in an attuned and contingent manner and then gradually *fading* so that the child does it for themselves (Claxton, 2002). This assistance could also be provided by peers in collaborative learning situations. These ideas link closely to the notion of *sustained shared thinking*. Sustained shared thinking is a process of engaged attention between two people as they work together to resolve a problem or develop an idea or skill (Siraj-Blatchford et al., 2002). The adult role within this can encompass a range of strategies to support the child such as showing a genuine interest, listening attentively, role modelling, asking open-ended questions, offering encouragement, making suggestions and/or clarifying ideas.

# Dimensions of learning

Deakin Crick (2006) developed the idea of Learning Power further and her work with Claxton and others identified various dimensions of learning that practitioners should acknowledge to develop a more effective ena-bling environment. This focuses on a learner's self-awareness of their learning, such as how they feel about learning, the learning relationships and the context of the learning experience. This draws upon the *ecology* of learning (Deakin Crick, 2006; Hutchings 2008) and examines factors such as the *climate* for learning within the setting, that is the conditions that enable effective learning to take place. This can be affected by, for example, the statutory curriculum or the setting's ethos, or by the values and beliefs the practitioner brings to the learning situation. All these factors will have an impact upon the child by the selection of what learning experiences are promoted and how they are supported. The wider cultural context of learning will also influence what is valued in terms of learning. For example, in learning about gender relationships, the influence of what is considered appropriate education and learning for different genders can vary across cultures and according to an individual's belief and value system.

Deakin Crick et al.'s (2004) research identified seven *dimensions of learning* which were considered important for all forms of learning, not just in a setting but in the wider world and for personal growth and development. The seven dimensions of learning were regarded as being on a continuum with polarised dimensions at either end of the scale. These are summarised in Table 9.2.

**Table 9.2** Dimensions of learning

| Dimension of learning | As opposed to . . . |
| --- | --- |
| Changing and learning | Being static |
| Critical curiosity | Being passive |
| Meaning making | Fragmentation |
| Creativity | Being rule bound |
| Learning relationships | Isolation and dependence |
| Strategic awareness | Being robotic |
| Resilience | Fragility and dependence |

Essentially, the dimensions explore approaches where the learning is learner-centred and the individual is proactive in taking responsibility for their own learning. They provide a sound framework for the examination of an individual's attitudes towards learning. Reflection was not included explicitly in the proposed dimensions although the individual has to assess themselves on the scale which does entail a degree of reflection. The seven dimensions combine *thinking, feeling and doing* and this underpins the development of Learning Power (Deakin Crick, 2006). Children are active participants in their own learning (*doing*). They *think* about their learning and examine how they *feel* about the learning tasks and situations. They then apply their new-found knowledge and implement change. This could involve approaching the tasks differently and *doing* them in a different way. These ideas link to the characteristics of effective learning identified in the EYFS and show how the Learning Power model can be related to early years contexts, as Table 9.3 demonstrates.

**Table 9.3** Characteristics of effective learning

| Characteristics of effective learning |
| --- |
| Active learning – motivation (FEELING) |
| – *Being involved and concentrating* |
| – *Keeping trying* |
| – *Enjoying achieving what they set out to do* |
| Creating and thinking critically – thinking (THINKING) |
| – *Having their own ideas* |
| – *Making links* |
| – *Choosing ways to do things* |
| Playing and exploring – engagement (DOING) |
| – *Finding out and exploring* |
| – *Playing with what they know* |
| – *Being willing to 'have a go'* |

*Source:* Early Education (2012).

---

**Mindful Moment**

Consider the seven dimensions of lifelong learning identified by Deakin Crick et al. (2004) which help to build Learning Power and compare these to the characteristics of effective learning. Can you find each of the seven dimensions within the various characteristics of effective learning? How do you help to build young children's Learning Power?

# The role of stress in developing resilience and self-efficacy

We have seen previously how new learning can excite and inspire but may also create a cognitive imbalance which generates a need to restore homeostasis in our brains and body (see Chapter 7 and Piaget's concept of *cognitive equilibrium*). Positive stress, or *eustress*, can be helpful as it pushes us to the limit and makes us more resourceful so that we develop our capacity to cope in adverse situations (see Chapter 3). It may only be when we are out of our comfort zone that our resources are really tested (Richards, 2011b). The novelty may generate a stress response such as anxiety, requiring down-regulation in order to learn effectively, but in order to learn we all need to be alert and responsive to the new stimulus.

The brain and body's need to establish homeostasis has implications for the practitioner role and how we support young children within the enabling environment. Earlier, we discussed some of the ways we can promote learning within the ZPD or *magic middle*. It is a contingent relationship that is fed by the child's responses, needs and interests. The early years practitioner needs to strike a careful balance between allowing a child to experiment and work things out for themselves and offering support when needed. However, our overarching aim is to promote emotional and cognitive self-regulation which will enhance a child's sense of achievement and self-efficacy. Ogden (2012) draws upon the work of Lazarus and Folkman, who identified self-efficacy as being instrumental in the coping mechanisms for alleviating and dealing with stress. Confidence in one's own abilities to cope with a stressful situation can lead to a reduction in the level of stress and therefore of the physical symptoms associated with stress. Ogden also cites Kobasa et al.'s notion of 'hardiness' which equates to Claxton's resilience. An individual displaying hardiness exhibits self-control, views problems and potential stressors as 'challenges' and displays commitment (Ogden, 2012).

## Mindful Moment

There is a well-known saying attributed to Niebuhr (1892–1971) which is to

'. . . grant me the serenity to accept the things I cannot change, the courage to change the things I can, and the wisdom to know the difference'.

What do you think of Neibuhr's saying – is it limiting or realistic? As early years practitioners we may have to make judgements about achieving a balance between setting attainable (often statutory) goals for the children, ones which are within reach and which they can realistically attain, and providing sufficient extension to enable them to reach their potential.

# Personality and resilience

Personality is the compilation of the character traits that evolve from your innate temperament and your life experiences. There has been much discussion and research about personality types such as Type A people who are driven to succeed, respond to time constraints and have a compulsion and determination to achieve goals and Type B people who are less goal-driven and more laid back (Ogden, 2012). There is considerable research (Straub, 2014) to suggest that being goal-driven could have detrimental health consequences, such as an increased susceptibility to developing cardiovascular disease, coronary heart disease (CHD) and high blood pressure which can be life-threatening. More recent research has focused on the degree of hostility or anger which has been linked to an increase in CHD. This indicates the importance of emphasising the process of self-regulation and empowering children so that they can deal with the stress in order to avoid potential harmful effects on their health in the future.

With the increasing *schoolification* of early years practice around the world, early years practitioners are often under pressure (or obligated by law) to help children achieve set goals (Rose and Rogers, 2012b). This can contribute to the tensions they face in deciding how to support young children's learning and development. This chapter has explored the importance of encouraging children to develop resilience and to increase their self-efficacy in respect of achieving their goals. However, it is equally as important to provide a balance so that they do not develop into adults that are so driven by their will to succeed that their actions become a way of life that may prove detrimental to their health.

## Key Points

- The health and well-being of children is linked to their ability to develop resilience and self-efficacy, which will enable them to withstand life's knocks.
- Learning Power can be developed and enables the child to take control of their own learning.
- Resourcefulness, reciprocity, relationships and resilience are key features in developing and Building Learning Power.
- The seven dimensions of Learning Power and the key characteristics of effective learning can provide a useful framework for analysing children's learning.
- Adults can work with the children to scaffold the development of resilience and help them to achieve cognitive and emotional equilibrium.

## Useful Further Reading and Websites

- Rose, J. and Rogers, S. (2012) *The Role of the Adult in Early Years Settings*. Maidenhead: Milton Keynes. This book provides an effective framework for considering your role within an early years setting and suggests ways to resolve some of the tensions within this role. 'The Facilitator' chapter is particularly useful for exploring how adults support young children in their learning.
- Claxton, G. (2002) *Building Learning Power*. Bristol: TLO Ltd. This book outlines the concept of Learning Power and how it can help practitioners to frame their practice and support young children to develop lifelong learning skills.
- Most children's charity websites have a section on resilience and are worth investigating for resources and clarification on the subject of resilience, for example Barnardo's at: http://www.barnardos.org.uk/.

# CHAPTER 10

# ECONOMIC AND SOCIAL FACTORS AFFECTING HEALTH AND WELL-BEING

## Chapter Overview

In this chapter we will focus on some of the economic and social factors that can affect children's health and well-being. Previously we have largely focused on the more intimate micro factors, such as personal relationships, experiences and environments, and how these combine and interact with genetic make-up and temperament to construct childhood experiences. Here, using poverty as our focus, we consider the influence of the larger context in which a child's world is situated. Examples of how macro factors, such as economic structures, physical environments and societal relations contribute to a child's health and well-being will be explored. With international recognition of the rights of every child there is a commitment to identify childhood as a stage in its own right and not just a transitional period to adulthood. Therefore we will explore how roles, rights and responsibilities are promoted and consider the importance of empowering children. In this way, we will gain a more holistic appreciation of the constructors and components of health and well-being, and so support practices that can both nurture and *sustain* health and well-being.

## Mindful Moment

Throughout this chapter keep in mind that as an individual we are *enmeshed* in *bidirectional relationships* with others, in our community and culture, and with our environment. As stated in the Introduction, by

*(Continued)*

*(Continued)*

adopting a bioecological view to child development (Bronfenbrenner, 2005) we recognise the *dynamic* relationships between national and international political, social and economic factors and look at their impact on children. Macro factors such as international laws, national health, education and care policies, and economic prosperity are translated into *local* service provision. It is the local service provision along with the quality and maintenance of local physical environments and community facilities and individual socio-cultural expectations about health and well-being that affect the child directly. So keep in mind that children, although their development appears unconnected to issues such as world peace and economic policy, are affected by them as they interact with a child's microsystems of families and social experiences.

# The rights of every child

There has been a growing global commitment to promoting better childhoods, and in 2000 the Millennium Development Goals (United Nations, 2014) were launched. These international goals are measurable, time-bound targets to reduce child mortality, eradicate poverty and hunger, attain universal primary education and achieve gender equity. Based on principles of human dignity and equality, they endorse a view of seeing childhood as a stage in its own right rather than a mere transitional phase to adulthood (Ben-Arieh, 2007). They are also driven by a shared belief that it is socially unacceptable and economically wasteful for there to be such inequalities in opportunities to access education and health services. It is suggested that it is culturally constructed social, legal and economic barriers that actually perpetuate the marginalisation of the most vulnerable in society, which include the poor, the disabled and the young (for a review see, for example, Boyden and Dercon, 2012; Fisher et al., 2014).

The United Nations Convention on the Rights of the Child (1989) (UNICEF, 2014b) was created to specifically focus and promote international human rights *for all children*. The United Kingdom signed the agreement in 1991, so all policies and programmes, including those related to the promotion of child health and well-being, have to ensure that children's rights are upheld. Article 27, for example, states that every child has the right to a standard of living that is *good enough* to meet their physical, social and mental needs, and governments have a responsibility to help all families who cannot afford to provide this. In England, there is an attempt to monitor the nation's well-being; however, the driving force behind this is unclear. Is this a social policy driven by moral or ethical motivation to improve life experiences or economic policy that recognises happier people achieve more at work and are therefore more likely to contribute to the community (Taylor, 2011)? Access to nurturing environments, adequate resources and relationships should neither be restricted nor considered a luxury, but *universal* and *fundamental* to all childhood experiences.

# Economic, social, human and cultural influences on child health and well-being

Boyden and Dercon (2012) advocate that childhood experience is so influential in shaping the adults we become that improving childhood experience is not only morally the right thing to do, but is also a necessity to support sustainable, national and international economic growth. Both the *availability* of economic, social and physical *resources*, referred to as *capitals*, and the *ability to access* them, influences a child's opportunity to achieve their potential. These *capitals* often combine and interact to provide *interconnected livelihood systems* that can support *or* compromise family life, and so directly influence a child's health and well-being.

The different kinds of capital that Obrist et al. (2010) believe influence health and well-being are described below.

## Human capital

This refers to the level of skills and knowledge an individual possesses. It is usually linked to levels of education and to work experience or professional status. Higher levels of educational attainment translate into higher human capital potential so, for example, jobs and higher salaries often depend on educational attainment. The amount of earning power you possess directly affects your ability to influence your health and well-being.

## Social capital

Social capital reflects the level of engagement, trust and reciprocity an individual has and shares with others. Social capital can be seen as the *strength* of the *connectivity* in personal networks and with other community networks. Those with higher social capital are well integrated into their community and have a close group of supportive friends and family. However, they also are connected to an extended group of other community members. These may include friends, colleagues, professionals and community service workers who have specific skills and can be relied upon for differing support needs.

## Cultural capital

Cultural capital is linked to social capital in that it refers to the *personal capacity* to use individual and community resources to achieve your goals and includes knowledge and understanding of cultural traditions. For example, those who move to live in another country may be disadvantaged because they are unaccustomed to cultural expectations and norms, and unaware of how to access community services and support. Another example may be first-time parents who are often unfamiliar with their role and lack expertise in caring for their child. If they do not have the cognitive capacity to learn skills in parenting, or know how to access the available support then their child's health and well-being may be compromised.

## Natural capital

The physical landscape and the availability of the natural environment, such as water and wildlife, are seen as natural capital. Decaying and overpopulated urban areas, with restricted access to wildlife habitats offer lower natural capital than areas that are open with access to natural spaces and clean air.

## Physical capital

Physical capital represents the availability and quality of transport networks, housing stock and energy supplies. Some rural areas have poorer physical capital in that there may be little affordable housing, limited public transport and few energy supply options. In contrast, purpose-built housing with facilities designed to support families, that are well served by local transport and access to employment, generate higher physical capital.

## Financial or economic capital

This relates to the materialistic resources that are available and includes personal savings and access to credit. Financial capital supports the purchase of basic and luxury services and products. It controls the amount that can be spent on food, buying new clothes, leisure experiences and paying for home rents or mortgages. In relation to parenting, higher economic capital means a greater ability to buy education, good health or leisure.

In society, it is *unequal access* to capitals that produces and perpetuates unfair advantage and disadvantage for children. In *poverty*, many hazards, including mental illness, racism, discrimination or unemployment can directly affect children but are also often beyond their parents'/carers' control (Balbernie, 2001).

### Mindful Moment

Consider how high levels of the six different types of capital could influence/affect parents/carers and a child's health and well-being.

Now complete the same exercise but consider how lower levels of the different types of capital may affect parents/carers and a child's health and well-being.

Why do you think poverty and lower levels of capital are linked?

# Poverty, deprivation and children's health and well-being

Although there are many macro factors, such as class, race and gender, that influence a child's future, *poverty* has enormous implications for children's health and well-being. The longer a child experiences poverty the greater is the legacy on their personal development

(Evans et al., 2011). Those who are born into and live in the most deprived communities will have the poorest mental and physical health and well-being and die on average 20 years earlier than the rest of the population (DoH, 2011b).

Poverty can be defined as absolute or relative (Shaw, 2010). *Absolute* poverty is when the family *income* is such that it is *insufficient* to provide the basic necessities of living, such as food, warmth and shelter. *Relative* poverty is defined in *relation to average incomes* and standards of living and is the more common form of poverty seen in England. Households in relative poverty have some income, but it is below *60 per cent* of the *national average income*. This means that basic necessities can be provided, but income is insufficient to allow full participation in society, leading to social exclusion and marginalisation (MacInnes et al., 2014). With national economic forces currently leading to sweeping cuts in social and welfare services, poverty is becoming increasingly concentrated into geographical areas that are already suffering from economic decline (Harkness et al., 2012). Some of the physical risk factors that are linked to poverty can also adversely affect health and well-being and include: substandard environmental conditions such as hazardous waste, water and air pollution, poor housing, poorly maintained schools with a high turnover of staff, high residential turnover, traffic congestion, poor community facilities such as neighbourhood sanitation, and higher levels of crime (Action for Children, 2014).

In poverty, *cycles of deprivation* and neglect can become established and perpetuate *intergenerational transmission of disadvantage* (Guy and Burghart, 2014). Deleterious economic and psychosocial well-being factors become increasingly connected, accumulating and compromising access to, and development of, personal and family capitals. Economic deprivation puts a child and their family on a trajectory for diminished educational and occupational attainment, educational failure, unemployment, severe personal debt, family breakdown and addiction. Sadly, in the Western world the biggest single cause of damage to an unborn baby's cognitive ability is parental alcohol abuse (BMA, 2007). As a consequence of psychosocial deprivation families show higher levels of: turmoil and violence, fragmented relationships and separation, lower levels of family cohesion and neglect, and increased illegal drug usage (Sadates and Dex, 2012). Although all physical, emotional and sexual abuse adversely affects child development, those who experience multiple abuse have higher levels of disruptive education experience and are involved in more disciplinary issues than those who experience neglect alone (McSherry, 2011). With inadequate access or provision to social and economic support, a family's ability to tolerate and survive adversity is eroded. This results in further challenges to the child/parent relationship and compromises to the stability of the family unit.

Deprivation is known to lead to an over-stimulation of the child's stress response system and this can alter their adaptive response capabilities (see Chapter 3). Chronic and extreme deprivation leads to a greater risk of developing anxiety, depression and cardiovascular problems later in life and can lead to a compromised ability to learn and to cope with adversity (Allen, 2011). Children who have been deprived of multi-sensory stimulation and nurturing environments can develop brain atrophy (shrinkage in certain areas of the brain that are under-stimulated, leading to reduced neuronal connections and activity). This is associated with an increase in risk for dissociative disorders and memory impairments (NSCDC, 2012). Indeed, in the UK, the Department of Health (2011b: 8) has identified a need to recognise the importance of childhood experience on mental health and well-being stating the following:

- One in ten children aged between 5 and 16 years has a mental health problem, with many continuing to have mental health problems into adulthood.
- Half of those with lifetime mental health problems first experience symptoms by the age of 14, and three-quarters before their mid-20s.

It is worth noting that, although statistical information gives us an indication of the scale of the problem, it should only be considered in relation to the research group context and cannot illustrate or represent individual experience.

# Risk and protective factors for health and well-being

Poverty and deprivation are not the only factors that can affect health and well-being. Table 10.1 summarises biological, environmental and social risk factors that can have an impact on mental health and well-being. It also shows the protective factors that can positively influence children's health and well-being (DfE, 2014b: 8–9). Many of the protective factors have been explored throughout this book and provide interesting insights into how practitioners can promote these in practice.

**Table 10.1** Biological, environmental and social dynamic factors that affect children's health and well-being

| | Risk factors | Protective factors |
|---|---|---|
| **In the child** | Genetic influences<br>Low IQ and learning disabilities<br>Specific development delay or neuro-diversity<br>Communication difficulties<br>Difficult temperament<br>Physical illness<br>Academic failure<br>Low self-esteem | Being female (in younger children)<br>Secure attachment experience<br>Outgoing temperament as an infant<br>Good communication skills, sociability<br>Being a planner and having a belief in control<br>Humour<br>Problem-solving skills and a positive attitude<br>Experiences of success and achievement<br>Faith or spirituality<br>Capacity to reflect |
| **In the family** | Overt parental conflict including domestic violence<br>Family breakdown (including where children are taken into care or adopted)<br>Inconsistent or unclear discipline<br>Hostile or rejecting relationships<br>Failure to adapt to a child's changing needs<br>Physical, sexual or emotional abuse<br>Parental psychiatric illness<br>Parental criminality, alcoholism or personality disorder<br>Death and loss – including loss of friendship | At least one good parent–child relationship (or one supportive adult)<br>Affection<br>Clear, consistent discipline<br>Support for education<br>Supportive long-term relationship or the absence of severe discord |
| **In the school** | Bullying<br>Discrimination<br>Breakdown in or lack of positive friendships<br>Deviant peer influences<br>Peer pressure<br>Poor pupil to teacher relationships | Clear policies on behaviour and bullying<br>'Open-door' policy for children to raise problems<br>A whole-school approach to promoting good mental health<br>Positive classroom management<br>A sense of belonging<br>Positive peer influences |
| **In the community** | Socio-economic disadvantage<br>Homelessness<br>Disaster, accidents, war or other overwhelming events<br>Discrimination<br>Other significant life events | Wider supportive network<br>Good housing<br>High standard of living<br>High morale school with positive policies for behaviour, attitudes and anti-bullying<br>Opportunities for valued social roles<br>Range of sport/leisure activities |

# Mindful Moment

Emmy Werner (Smith et al., 2011) carried out a longitudinal study over forty years on the Hawaiian island of Kauai. The research revealed that some individuals could, despite physical disadvantage and deprived childhoods, succeed and go on to be highly successful. The research focused on 698 infants born in 1955 who were followed until they were 40 years old.

Of the children, 422 were born without complications and grew up in supportive environments and stable relationships. The others experienced degrees of disadvantage and neglect which included parental pre-natal stress, chaotic and disadvantaged homes, and uneducated or alcoholic or mentally unstable parents. Many of the children grew up having health problems and, at 40 years old, felt ineffectual and helpless. However, despite adverse environmental and relational experiences *a small number* of children became competent adults who were able to find work, integrated well with others and contributed to their communities. Werner noted that these individuals seemed to be *resilient* to their childhood adversity. They shared the following experiences or characteristics:

- Had at least one close bond with a caregiver who accepted them unconditionally and gave them positive attention during their early years. The attachment figure was not always the parent, but included grandparents, siblings, aunts and uncles or regular babysitters.
- Temperamental characteristics included being active, sociable and a low degree of excitability and distress. They were seen by peers and adults as easy going, even tempered and affectionate.
- Teachers noted they concentrated in class, were alert, responsive, physically active and excelled at sports.
- They were adept at seeking out supportive adults when their parents were unable to support them.
- They had a positive outlook and seemed to be able to take advantage of support networks and adults in the community and school.
- Schools were perceived as a refuge from their dysfunctional family life, and teachers were turned to in times of crisis.

Why do you think these factors/experiences were *protective*?

In what ways do you think families, early years professionals, communities and nations should support high-risk children to try to break intergenerational disadvantage?

# Roles and responsibilities in promoting children's health and well-being

In response to extensive research evidence and growing concern about the consequences of poverty on health and well-being, the Child Poverty Act was passed in 2010 in the UK. This made it a statutory duty for any government to end child poverty by 2020/21. The act established four separate child poverty targets to be met by 2020/21. All governments, including those in Scotland and Northern Ireland, are required to publish a regular Child Poverty Strategy and an annual progress report. A Child Poverty Commission has been created to coordinate strategies and provide advice, while local authorities and other community delivery partners must evidence working together to tackle child poverty. Most importantly the Act stipulates that children and families are given a voice by actively involving them in developing strategies to end child poverty (Save the Children, 2014). The hope is that the Child Poverty Act not only ensures national services work together to eliminate the unfair disadvantage that poverty bestows on families and children but also builds a society that *feels responsible* and *empowered* to contribute to sustainable health and well-being.

Although responsive relationships are 'developmentally expected and biologically essential' (NSCDC, 2012: 1), up to 80 per cent of neglected children show evidence of some form of attachment difficulty, compromising their ability to form ongoing lasting relationships (Action for Children, 2014). Currently 23 per cent of the UK's ill-health is categorised as mental rather than physical and £2 billion is annually spent on social care for people with mental health problems although the cost of treating these problems could double over the next 20 years (DoH, 2011b: 10). Therefore, the government has both an economic and a moral duty to focus on the promotion of personal and collective practices to promote better health and well-being, particularly for those identified as vulnerable. The need, particularly for children identified as vulnerable, is for both early intervention strategies and continuing support strategies. This would improve health and well-being, help prevent mental illness and reduce costs resulting from ill health, unemployment or antisocial behaviours (DoH, 2011b; Marmot, 2010). Some of these ideas are revisited in the next chapter.

## Key Points

- Human, social and economic capitals can nurture or constrain development and change over a lifespan.
- There is a range of personal and environmental risk and protective factors that affect health and well-being.
- When a child is born into poverty often multiple factors cluster together with adverse consequences on psychological health and well-being.
- There needs to be an all-party political recommitment to the United Nations Convention on the Rights of the Child (UNCRC, 1989) to support and sustain children's rights to have access to and be involved in their health and well-being.

# Useful Further Reading and Websites

- You can read more about the UNCRC (1989) at: http://www.unicef.org/crc/.
- You can find more about child poverty in the UK and the relationship between economic and social factors on poverty and neglect from the website at: http://www.endchildpoverty.org.uk/.

# CHAPTER 11

# EARLY INTERVENTION IN HEALTH AND WELL-BEING

---

## Chapter Overview

In this chapter we build on the discussion on macro factors that affect health and well-being by considering the notion of early intervention and its implications for young children's health and well-being. It will consider the concept of early intervention, global perspectives on its process and the impact of early trauma. The chapter will also highlight some key early intervention initiatives that are attempting to foster health and well-being in the early years. Two key issues surrounding the promotion of health and well-being in practice are also explored – the importance of practitioner well-being and the significance of having a team around the child to support this work.

---

## Early intervention

The World Health Organisation considers early childhood development to be an 'important phase in life which determines the quality of health, well-being, learning and behaviour across the life span' (WHO, 2014). The significance of the early years in laying foundations for lifelong emotional and physical health and well-being is borne out by the wealth of evidence from a range of disciplines – neuroscience, developmental psychology, education and economics (Melhuish, 2014). These benefits extend into cognitive, educational and social development. Studies show, for example, how educational outcomes can be predicted at 22 months and criminal behaviour at three years, and how many mental health difficulties are attributed to adverse early experiences (Allen, 2011). Indeed, UNICEF (2013b) states that the 'early years of childhood form the basis of intelligence, personality, social behaviour, and capacity to learn and nurture oneself as an adult'. UNICEF (2013b) also draws attention to the range of evidence to demonstrate why and how a good foundation has lifelong and intergenerational repercussions, and well as having an impact on the financial and social capital of societies.

Recognition of the significance of the early years has led to worldwide attention being directed towards early childhood education and care and the need to intervene early to get the best possible start in life. A recent report by the Centre for Excellence and Outcomes identifies early intervention as a 'force for transforming the lives of children, families and communities, particularly the most disadvantaged', citing the evidence of personal, social and economic benefits (C4EO, 2010: 3). The World Health Organisation also cites conclusive evidence to show how early and appropriate interventions that address risk factors, such as those identified in the previous chapter, can help to improve health and well-being in young children and calls for early intervention to be integrated into national and international policies aimed at improving health equality. From the perspective of economics, the work of Nobel economist James Heckman (2011) is increasingly cited in favour of early intervention, which shows how the rates of return on economic investment in the early years can yield the greatest returns in terms of human capital.

A recent UK report called for a culture of early intervention to permeate policy and practice in government and within children's services. In this report, early intervention was defined as 'general approaches, and the specific policies and programmes, which help to give children the social and emotional bedrock they need to reach their full potential' (Allen, 2011: vii). We also saw in the previous chapter how particular attention is being paid to young children from disadvantaged backgrounds and how early intervention might help to break the cycle of inequalities in health, education and employment to improve outcomes. In early intervention, the focus moves away from addressing *symptoms* to alleviating the *causes* of inequality and recognising that later interventions are less effective in tackling such issues (Marmot, 2010). Similar drives are evident elsewhere in the world (Blackman, 2002; UNICEF, 2013b). One such issue is the impact of trauma in the early years and its implications for health and well-being, as the next section considers.

> **Mindful Moment**
>
> Think about the evidence base for the idea of early intervention pre-sented in this chapter and from elsewhere in the book. If someone were to ask you why and how early years experience lays the foundation for lifelong health and well-being, what would you say? How do you see your role in this?

# Trauma in the early years

Like most terms trauma can be defined in many different ways but the word originates from the Greek word meaning injury. The World Health Organisation defines trauma in early childhood as adverse early experiences, such as unstable caregiving, deprivation of love or nutrition, neglect or maltreatment (WHO, 2014). Trauma might also relate to incidents that occur within a child's experience that are unintentional and unrelated to abuse or neglect, such as the death of a relative, transitions, family breakdown or physical illness (O'Connor and Russell, 2004). In turn, families may be under structural, economic, social and political pressures and circumstances, which may affect their capacity to support a child's physical and emotional health and well-being.

Clearly, there is a *spectrum of trauma* which is affected by the nature, duration and interpersonal context of the incident/s (Glaser, 2000). In relation to the psychoneurobiological model of human development, trauma relates to acquired brain injury resulting from unregulated stress (Cairns, 2001). Traumatic events, whatever their origin, are often stored in the brain and body as implicit memories when experienced in the first few years of life. Toxic stress can produce 'physiological disruptions or biological "memories" that undermine the development of the body's stress response systems and affect the developing brain, cardiovascular system, immune system, and metabolic regulatory controls' (NSCDC, 2010: 1). Children may later experience these memories as *physical* or *emotional sensations* producing flashbacks, nightmares or other uncontrollable reactions of which they have no conscious, working memory (Applegate and Shapiro, 2005). Earlier chapters have also made reference to the evidence that young children who experience extreme stress are at greater risk of developing a range of cognitive, social and/or emotional difficulties (UNICEF, 2013b). A recent NSPCC review of evidence shows that:

> Child abuse or neglect and general trauma, including witnessing violence, alter normal child development and, without intervention, can have lifelong consequences. We now have evidence that such early adversities also make adults more vulnerable to stress and stress-related conditions such as cardiovascular disease and substance abuse. (2011: 14)

Cairns (2001) notes how trauma disrupts physiological, psychological and social functioning and identifies three key areas where traumatised children have particular difficulty – in *self-regulating stress*, in *processing information* about the world and their own *inner feelings* and in difficulties *making and maintaining relationships*.

One study demonstrates that nearly all children will have experienced some kind of trauma by the end of their primary years (O'Connor and Russell, 2004). We also saw in Chapter 5 how unmet attachment needs can affect between 30 and 40 per cent of children, which in turn affects learning and behaviour (Bergin and Bergin, 2009). Other research suggests that 80 per cent of children diagnosed with ADHD have attachment issues, raising some interesting questions about developmental trauma and its impact (Clarke et al., 2002; Moss and St-Laurent, 2001). The previous chapter highlighted that there is greater prevalence of attachment difficulties in disadvantaged families and children with disorganised attachment are likely to emerge from more chaotic families, particularly those who experience what has been dubbed the *toxic trio*. The toxic trio is substance misuse, domestic abuse and mental ill-health, which invariably result in developmental trauma, particularly via maltreatment (i.e. emotional abuse, neglect or physical harm), and the three elements occur in about 35 per cent of child protection cases (NSPCC, 2011). Horton notes that 'maltreatment is one of the biggest paediatric public-health challenges' (2003: 443).

It is also important to remember that trauma comes in many forms and can affect all children across all socio-economic groups – for example, 'boarding school syndrome' has been identified among more privileged groups by clinicians who show how boarding school experiences can have a negative and often serious impact on health and well-being that persists well into adulthood (Schaverien, 2011). Maternal depression also affects all socio-economic groups (Entwistle, 2013). Overall, most early years practitioners are likely to encounter at least some insecurely attached and traumatised children in their setting. Article 39 of the UNCRC states that governments should take all appropriate measures to promote the physical and psychological recovery and social reintegration of traumatised children. The following case study provides an interesting example of how the early intervention strategy of Theraplay might support a child who has experienced early trauma by not have their attachment needs met effectively.

## Case Study

### Supporting traumatised children

Suzie was a three-year-old girl who was displaying challenging behaviours in her nursery and at home. She had very poor social skills and would react disproportionately to seemingly minor triggers. Suzie had such a strong need to be in control that the nursery environment was impossible for her to manage and the placement broke down due to episodes of violence against herself, adults and other children. A package of support was offered that included Theraplay with parent and child and one-on-one therapeutic childcare sessions for Suzie.

Theraplay is an attachment-based intervention that uses play based on the natural interactions between infant and caregiver in healthy 'good enough' relationships. Initial assessments revealed that the intervention would need to support Suzie and her parents to strengthen their attachment relationship by modelling attunement to Suzie's emotional needs, helping Suzie to accept and enjoy positive touch as a way of connecting to people, and providing opportunities to co-regulate so that Suzie could use more positive strategies to self-regulate.

After 12 months of weekly sessions, there were strong improvements. Suzie was happier and calmer, was able to verbalise feelings and take turns in play, was able to enjoy massages and allow the adult to take the lead more peacefully. The parents felt Theraplay had supported them to understand Suzie and her needs better. Suzie's comments showed increased positive self-regard – 'I can do this, can't I?' – and also showed how she had developed an understanding of nurturing touch and could enact this in her own behaviour – 'I smoothed the cat until she calmed down.'

(Alison, Theraplay therapist and inclusion support worker for children with social, emotional and behavioural needs)

## Policy initiatives

There are clear economic drivers behind political policy relating to early intervention within many countries given that early intervention investments are dramatically more cost-effective and efficient than later remedial interventions (Allen, 2011; Paterson, 2011). Within this imperative is a particular emphasis on improving educational outcomes and ensuring school readiness (DfE, 2013; UNICEF, 2013b). Such initiatives are invariably coated in egalitarian dogma of breaking intergenerational cycles of inequality. Nonetheless, it is fair to say that, at least rhetorically, such policies have been influenced by the key principles within the UNCRC, as seen in the previous chapter. The advantages to society of early intervention policy initiatives are therefore driven by a range of imperatives to benefit all, but one aim is to help young children experience a better quality of life in their earliest years, thereby promoting their long-term health and well-being.

A well-known policy initiative in England is the Sure Start policy implemented in the late 1990s and early 2000s. This enterprise was strongly influenced by the Head Start programme in the US. From its inception the Sure Start programme was designed to bring together health, education and social welfare services at a local level. It focused on developing appropriate and integrated services which might include early years provision, social services functions, health services, training and employment services, and information and advice services. Sure Start centres became a statutory requirement and the original targeted approach was extended to a more ambitious aim to develop universal provision through the establishment of Children's Centres throughout the country from 2007. However, a change in government and economic austerity led to a shrinkage of this expansion plan and a re-focus on targeted areas and families. Currently, the core purpose of Children's Centres is to improve outcomes, increase school readiness and reduce inequalities in areas of greatest need (DfE, 2013). Moreover, the intention is that Children's Centres should act as a hub for the local community, building social capital and cohesion, as well as provide access to affordable early years education and childcare via the universal provision of pre-school care for two to four year olds and targeted provision for disadvantaged two year olds (DfE, 2013). Although there have been mixed findings from the Sure Start evaluations, longer-term studies have shown numerous improvements in, for example, children's behaviour, the home learning environment and increase of service use. These improvements, however, are inconsistent with a variation of results across the country highlighting some of the challenges of ensuring consistent early intervention strategies for all young children (Melhuish, 2014).

Another example of a policy initiative related to early intervention in England is the Healthy Child Programme (HCP) (DoH, 2009). The HCP is an early intervention and prevention public health programme and is a universal service for children and families and correlates with the Health and Social Care Act 2012. This Act established Health and Well-being Boards in local authorities as a forum whereby local health and care systems could together improve the health and well-being of their local population and reduce health inequalities. Part of this process includes creating integrated early intervention approaches, such as the work of Health Visitors. Health Visitors are an integral part of the programme and work closely with early years professionals and other multi-agency teams in supporting young children and their families from birth to five years. Health Visitors also help to ensure that more vulnerable children receive appropriate referral to specialist services, and to signpost families for wider support with the ultimate aim of tackling inequality. Their work was expanded in 2011 under the Coalition government (DoH/NHS, 2013) and under the new Health Visitor programme every child and their family are entitled to new birth visits, advice on health, physical and development checks, and general support. Later in this chapter we look at another policy initiative which is operated by Health Visitors and early years practitioners, namely the two-year-old health check.

The Health Visitor system resonates with the Start4Life initiative aimed at supporting pregnancy and the first year of a child's life within the health services (DoH, 2009, 2014). The following case study illustrates a more targeted move towards improving health and well-being for more vulnerable families that was first developed in America and is now being used as an early intervention strategy in Britain and complements the Health Visitor programme.

## Case Study

### The Family Nurse Partnership

Angela is a Family Nurse who is implementing the Family Nurse Partnership model in England. She writes:

The Family Nurse Partnership (FNP) is an evidence-based intensive home visiting programme for first-time teenage mothers. It is a preventative voluntary programme delivered in pregnancy until the child is two years old by specially trained Family Nurses. The FNP was introduced into Britain in 2007 having evolved from 30 years of research and clinical trials in the US (DoH, 2012). The programme aims to improve pregnancy outcomes, child health and development, and encourage economic independence and healthy relationships (Olds et al., 1997). As a Family Nurse many of the people with whom I work are extremely vulnerable, often with dysfunctional family relationships and disorganised attachment behaviours, poor academic achievement, poor physical, emotional and psychological health and low self-esteem. The Family Nurse intervenes at a time when the young person is motivated for change due to an intrinsic desire to do the best for their baby. The FNP programme is a structured model that is predicated upon a therapeutic nurse–client relationship. By enabling the young person to develop trust and form attachment-type behaviours with their nurse (within professional boundaries), they can then model this within their own relationships and most importantly build a positive relationship with their baby, with the resultant secure attachment, encouraging maximum positive brain connections to enable the baby's optimum health. The self-efficacy element within the programme is also of significance. I have found that enabling them to make small positive changes/achieve a small goal, provides them with the feel-good factor, a feeling of success and achievement. In turn, this raises confidence and self-worth, encouraging them to be more assertive in making positive health behaviour choices, seek access to services, and be more emotionally and physically available and responsive to their child. There can be other positive outcomes as well – one client is now doing midwifery training and another doing a degree in Early Years Education.

(Angela, Family Nurse, Children, Young People and Family Support Centre)

## The team around the child

Health Visiting and the Family Nurse Partnership are premised on effective multi-agency working. This is a fundamental necessity for effective early intervention. Indeed, we have seen from the examples of policy initiatives the overwhelming emphasis on integrated services that is required if provision for universal health and well-being is to be effectively achieved. The evidence suggests that the greater the inter-agency collaboration, the greater the improvements in positive outcomes for children and their families (Melhuish, 2014; NSPCC, 2011). An integrated service model which helps to establish a team around the child (Siraj-Blatchford et al., 2007) reflects the spirit of shared responsibility and communal effort. This resonates with the well-known saying that it takes a village to raise a child, whereby the responsibility for raising a child is shared with the larger family and wider community. Blackman (2002) has shown how family support and coordinated community involvement are key to the success of early intervention. Indeed, caregiver and community capacities to promote health and well-being rely on the social capital provided by neighbourhoods, organisations, early years professionals, family and linked associations, including the parents' workplaces, to provide a supportive role in strengthening the process (NSCDC, 2010).

A recent example of integrated working is the introduction of the health check for two year olds in England as part of the Healthy Child Programme. This policy is designed to ensure early assessment of young children in order to promote positive outcomes in health and well-being, including identifying any intervention needs that may be necessary (IRDG, 2013). All early years practitioners are required to conduct a progress check at age two for their key children. This is the age which is considered by the government to be where apparent difficulties in areas of development, such as language and behaviour, can become evident (NCB, 2012). It essentially comprises a short, written summary of a child's development and is meant to concentrate on the three prime learning and development areas of the EYFS: Personal, Social and Emotional Development; Physical Development; and Communication and Language (DfE, 2014a). The aim of the health check is to provide information for parents and practitioners in order to identify needs and to report on any areas where progress is less than expected and, if so, to identify a plan of action for referral to other services which may provide additional support. The health check is to be undertaken in collaboration with the child, the family and other early intervention professionals, such as the health visitor. Moreover, it intends to bring together health and education in order to provide a more complete picture of the child combining the knowledge of how children are learning and developing alongside the expertise of a health professional (NCB, 2012). It therefore adopts a *bioecological systems model* of integrated working and operates on Bronfenbrenner's (1979) principle of multiperson systems of interaction.

Indeed, throughout this book we have emphasised that the core theme for health and well-being is via the establishment of *quality relationships*. Integrated working hinges upon effective relationship building, not just between practitioner and child but between practitioner and the family, and with other professionals. Perry's work with traumatised children also highlighted the benefits of a community-based approach (Perry and Szlavitz, 2006). He refers to the ongoing network of support that can be as, if not more, important for vulnerable children than one-to-one interventions that might only last an hour a week. As Cozolino (2013: 7) notes:

Studies of high risk children and adolescents who show resilience in the face of trauma and stress often report one or two adults that took a special interest in them and became invested in their success.

Sroufe and Siegel (2011) also emphasise the evidence which suggests that a network of supportive relationships can help more vulnerable children to make changes in their internal working models. A network of support can help also help to manage caregiver/practitioner stress as the following section highlights (Entwhistle, 2013). The following case study is an example of a support network and interagency collaboration that was developed to create nurturing services for children.

## Case Study

### The team around the child – Nurture Outreach

This case study reviews a Nurture Outreach strategy developed by a local authority in England in order to better support the needs of young children moving from the relative small-based, high-ratio staffing of early years settings to schools, in particular those children with social, emotional and attachment needs.

The Nurture Outreach service was developed through involvement and consultation with a number of primary schools, social care, Children and Adolescent Mental Health Services, school nursing, behaviour outreach services, the voluntary sector and early years. The strategy was to monitor the rise in needs and consider new approaches to supporting children's needs in school. The service included the appointment of a Theraplay practitioner for children with complex emotional and behavioural needs, a dedicated educational psychologist and a parent support advisor. It also included attachment-aware and trauma-informed training for all staff (teachers, teaching assistants, SENCos and head teachers) to learn new strategies and approaches to best meet the needs of these children. Pilot evaluations of the study have shown that nurturing approaches in the broadest sense can support children's social, emotional and behavioural development and learning. For example, improvements have been recorded in relation to children's capacity to self-regulate their behaviour with a consequent drop in support needed by staff. The strategy seeks to promote a holistic approach to supporting children, building on their strengths as well as identifying any needs.

(Sara, Children's Services service manager)

## Practitioner well-being

The idea of a network of support being essential for children's health and well-being (NICE, 2012) is also true for the practitioners who work with them. Melhuish (2014) emphasises the role of practitioners in creating high-quality early childhood education and care by improving children's daily experience, particularly for more vulnerable children from disadvantaged homes. It is a complex, challenging and demanding role requiring a wide range of attributes, knowledge and skills (Rose and Rogers, 2012a). In England, along with the various statutory requirements of the EYFS, the relentless pace of policy change and the perceived menace of Ofsted inspections make the burdens of the busy practitioner are a heavy load to bear. In addition to the day-to-day tensions of ascertaining what support might be appropriate for children, Rose and Rogers (2012b) identified several layers of pressure on early years practitioners from parents, colleagues and the government, which often create emotional and cognitive dissonance for practitioners when these demands are conflict with their principles about quality early education. Practitioner stress is also directly affected by the nature of the relationship they have with the children (Spilt et al., 2011). Moreover, a practitioner may be experiencing personal stress within their own life that may affect their capacity to perform effectively.

Recent research on well-being in early years settings demonstrates that 'practitioners' well-being is a pre-requisite for effectively supporting children's well-being' (Manning-Morton, 2014: 148). We saw, for example, in Chapters 6 and 9 the importance of the adult's emotional intelligence and capacity to self-regulate their own stresses in order to be an effective co-regulator (Schore, 2001b). Our sense of professional identity, job satisfaction and staff morale are an important basis for ensuring practitioners feel valued and are motivated to perform effectively, which in turn affects performance and retention (Bradford, 2012). Given that young children require 'continuity, consistency and constancy', such factors need to be taken into consideration when promoting health and well-being of children (Manning-Morton and Thorp, 2003: 177). Bradford (2012) also draws attention to the need for a balanced reward: effort ratio to occur within our daily working lives in order to ensure our well-being and happiness. Such potential imbalance raises the importance of ensuring an effective network of support for practitioners working with young children.

## Mindful Moment

Manning-Morton makes the following comments about some of the tensions and challenges facing early years practitioners:

> Early years practitioners need to engage with the darker side of children's learning and developing, with their distress, their defiance, their dependency and their inherent mess and chaos. This is a major professional challenge for early years practitioners, as engaging closely with young children touches deeply held personal values and often deeply buried personal memories . . . [Moreover,] the constant 'giving' that this entails means that their 'jug' of emotional resources can easily run dry, leading to self-protective measures that include disconnecting from work relationships, high levels of sickness, and staff turnover. (2014: 152, 154)

How does this quote resonate with your own perspectives of the professional challenges in working with young children?

Think more generally about your own work experiences. How do they affect your health and well-being? Think about any factors that make you feel valued, motivated and satisfied by the job, and those that may do the opposite?

The National Institute for Health and Care Excellence advocates an organisation-wide approach to promoting well-being (NICE, 2009) and Manning-Morton (2014) highlights the importance of personal and professional support in order to ensure practitioner well-being. One of the most effective ways to help practitioners to maintain healthy emotional well-being is to provide a professional forum for discussing well-being issues, moderating stress levels and sharing stressful encounters, such as the practice of regular supervision meetings. In England, supervision is now enshrined in the EYFS as a statutory requirement (DfE, 2014a). The practice of supervision can provide a safe space away from the demanding work environment to give practitioners opportunities for reflection, collaboration and problem-solving, and a team-building context for exploring professional and personal self-development issues in order to enhance well-being and improve practice (Blase and

Blase, 2004). Supervision can also promote a culture of participation, equality and fairness which can induce a greater sense of harmony among staff. The following case study provides an interesting example of how mindfulness is being used within supervision programmes in one local authority.

## Case Study

### Mindfulness Supervision

Heidi is a Children's Centre service manager. In this case study, she talks about her experiences of leading Mindfulness Supervision sessions as part of the support programme for her staff in order to improve their collective health and well-being.

> Within family support work, practitioners (Children's Centre workers, health visitors, social workers) are often supporting parents with complex unresolved attachment issues. Practitioners will often find themselves needing to act as parent in the parent–child relationship – offering reciprocity, containment and support for an array of feelings or emotions. For the protection of the practitioner and to enable an open, honest and transparent relationship, s/he must be supported to self-regulate and manage stress if family support work is to be most effective and burn-out is to be prevented. To support this, we introduced fortnightly mindfulness sessions for our staff into our working week. These included mindfulness practices such as mindful breathing exercises, mindful movement and mindful meditation as part of our supervision support.
>
> Practitioners expressed feeling more appreciative and aware of changes within their body in the face of stressful interactions and more able to contain and use them to encourage parents to reflect on the impact their behaviour was having or could have on others. Those more regularly undertaking mindfulness exercise outside of these times described feeling calmer, more in control and with improved sleep patterns.
>
> I feel mindful practice is crucial in supporting parents to be the best parents they can be, enabling them to take the most they can from formal and informal parenting support and programmes and ultimately reduce the widening attainment gap.
>
> (Heidi, Children's Centre service manager)

Roberts (2010) extends the idea of individual practitioner well-being to the notion of collective well-being and universal well-being and the need for a collective response as a society to ensure social justice, to develop cross-cultural caring and understanding, and to have a sense of belonging to a greater whole. These ideas are explored in our final, concluding chapter which considers the sustainability of health and well-being.

---

## Key Points

- There is overwhelming evidence from a variety of sources and disciplines that testifies to the value of early intervention for health and well-being.
- Adverse early experiences necessitate the intervention of early years practitioners and multi-agency professionals in helping to ameliorate the impact of early trauma.
- There are numerous global and national initiatives that seek to implement early intervention strategies in policy and practice.
- The team around the child and inter-agency collaborative working at an international, national and local level is an essential component of effective early intervention strategies.
- Practitioner well-being also plays an integral role in generating health and well-being in young children, and settings should provide a range of supportive mechanisms to help maintain a reasonable reward: effort balance within the workplace and beyond.

---

# Useful Further Reading and Websites

- C4EO (Centre for Excellence in Outcomes) (2010) *Grasping the Nettle: Early Intervention for Children, Families and Communities*. Available at: https://www.family-action.org.uk/wp-content/uploads/2014/06/early_intervention_grasping_the_nettle_full_report.pdf (accessed 11 December 2014). This provides a useful overview of the evidence relating to early intervention and a practice guide in supporting children, families and communities.
- Manning-Morton, J. (ed.) (2014) *Exploring Well-being in the Early Years*. Maidenhead: Open University Press. This is a valuable book which covers a range of issues related to well-being and the different ways well-being is experienced within early years practice.

- A useful charity organisation which provides evidence and advice on early intervention in the UK is the Early Intervention Foundation website at: http://www.eif.org.uk/.
- Another useful source of information which provides up-to-date information and support for early years practitioners in England is the Foundation Years website at: http://www.foundationyears.org.uk/.

# CHAPTER 12

# CONCLUSION: SUSTAINABLE HEALTH AND WELL-BEING

---

## Chapter Overview

In this final and concluding chapter we begin by outlining a framework for promoting sustainable health and well-being in young children from birth onwards. This framework, called Five to Thrive, is an example of an accessible and effective early intervention approach that operates within a bioecological systems model by helping multi-agency professionals in their work with young children and families. It draws on psychoneuro-biological research that enables children to experience progressively more complex interactions and activities to advance their social, emotional and cognitive development, and to increase their capacity to become agents of their own learning. It illustrates the key themes developed throughout this book including the significance of relationships and addresses the common tensions facing practitioners and caregivers in developing a balanced pedagogy. The chapter ends with some final comments related to sustainability in health and well-being.

---

## Five to Thrive – a framework for promoting health and well-being

Five to Thrive is a framework of five key activities which are essentially building blocks for a healthy brain (Cairns, 2014). Cairns created the Five to Thrive approach as food for the brain and it consists of the following five key activities:

**Respond · Engage · Relax · Play · Talk**

Five to Thrive has been endorsed by the Social Mobility and Child Poverty Commission as an effective programme for early intervention (SMCPC, 2014) and the Centre for Excellence and Outcomes in Children and Young People's Services (C4EO). An evaluation report demonstrated the effectiveness of the simplicity, clarity and accessibility of the Five to Thrive messages. Its flexibility meant that it could be implemented by a variety of agencies and practitioners in a myriad of ways, and it has shown itself to be a successful and low-cost approach for improving practice in work with families and young children (Ghate et al., 2013).

The Five to Thrive activities follow a neuro-sequencing process. In this respect the framework is based on the *psychoneurobiological* model of human development. In other words, the activities have been designed to work with the brain and body to help build the mind, and to work with the sensory and nervous system to forge helpful connections between the limbic system and the frontal lobes. These activities are explored briefly in the sections that follow, particularly the Engage activity, since the attunement process and interactional synchrony largely hinge upon what kind of engagement is undertaken. The framework is thus also based on a relational model in the spirit of the *bioecological* systems model and can be used by practitioners/caregivers to ascertain suitable intercessions in their work with young children. Indeed, Cairns (2014) offers two key processes that inform a practitioner's engagement with young children and these will be discussed first.

## Soothing and stimulating – two key processes

In previous chapters, we have seen that one of the main challenges for practitioners is knowing what action might be needed (or not) in order to help and support a child's health and well-being (including their cognitive learning). A helpful way to think about what to do, Cairns suggests, is to consider any prospective interaction with a child as either a *soothing* process or a *stimulation* process. A stimulation activity is aiming to up-regulate a child's arousal system, that is to increase their interest and engagement by stimulating the sensory and nervous systems responsible for progressing learning. On the other hand, a 'soothing' activity is designed to down-regulate a child's arousal, to calm and enable the sensory and nervous systems to restore balance in the brain and body either to enable recovery time (such as sleeping) or perhaps to reduce the child to levels more receptive to stimulating learning experiences (such as resolving a problem so that they can continue playing) (Schore, 2014). Finding a delicate balance between the *see-saw* of soothing and stimulating experiences and knowing *when* and *how* to initiate, sustain and/or terminate a soothing or stimulating activity is a pivotal part of the early years practitioner's practice.

---

### Mindful Moment

We have seen that finding a balance between the see-saw of soothing and stimulation processes might help to simplify how we might interpret our interactions and enable us to make decisions about how to engage with children.

Think about the see-saw of soothing and stimulating activities in your own practice or in practice you have witnessed – what actions sit on the soothing side of the see-saw and which on the stimulating side?

## Respond

The *Respond* activity is essentially based on our innate need to be noticed and begins the social engagement process by switching on the adult's brain to make a connection to the child. For a young baby, this is fundamental for their survival since they are entirely reliant on an adult responding to their needs. Cairns refers to the *Respond* activity as loving attention and highlights that as soon as we turn our attention in a responsive way to the child, their sensory and nervous system responds in turn – as Cairns (2014) puts it, the adult *feeds* the child and the child *exercises* in response. Shonkoff refers to this as the *serve and return* of mutually rewarding interactions which lay down essential prerequisites for the development of healthy brain circuits and increasingly complex skills, laying foundations for life (NSCDC, 2010). The *Respond* activity involves being attuned and sensitive in the ways that we have explored elsewhere in order to promote interactional synchrony. As such we need to 'perceive, make sense of, and respond in a timely and effective manner to the actual moment-to-moment signals sent by the child' (Sroufe and Siegel, 2011: 2).

## Engage

This activity is about what we *do* (or not do!) after we have responded (noticed) a child's need or interest. The actions we take help to switch on the child's brain to the social engagement system and connect with the adult. It is essentially about positive engagement which might come in the form of a loving touch or some kind of proximity behaviour. This notion links closely to one of Bowlby's (1969) key tenets of attachment theory – the need to be in close proximity with the secure base of the attachment figure. Much of young children's behaviour centres on this need. The action that gets taken within this key activity will depend on the child's internal mental and physical state. It might only entail a glance or perhaps just a 'wait and see' stance, where we *actively do nothing* in order to initiate a child's sense of agency and enable them to navigate their own way forward. If a child is distressed, then clearly the engaging activity will need to be one that will take the child on a journey to relax. Invariably, the engagement activity involves touch. Research has demonstrated our need for affectionate touch and the positive effects of appropriate touch on our physical and emotional health and well-being (Entwistle, 2013), which can come in many different forms – massaging, stroking, patting, holding hands. Schore (2014) refers to the idea of *touch synchrony* which is where a caregiver/practitioner and child communicate through interpersonal touch and can alter vagal tone and cortisol activity in a positive way. Moreover, touch can also be used as a stimulating, playful activity, such as tickling and bouncing. It is also important to note that the *Engage* activity need not necessitate actual physical contact – just being in the same space, even if you are doing different activities, might be sufficient to support the child in that moment. It might also entail just mimicking the child and adjusting to their rhythms via mirroring activities. We saw in earlier chapters the significant role that mirror neurons play in a child's development and the mirroring process. Watson (1996) discusses the *sociobiological feedback system* that is involved in the mirroring process which enables children to feel and know that their feelings are understood and can be contained. In this way, the caregiver/practitioner helps to establish *physical attunement* with the child (Cairns, 2014).

## Relax

The *Relax* activity might entail taking more proactive steps to soothe a child and relax them and helps to establish *emotional attunement* (Cairns, 2014). The most notable example is cuddling. We have also seen in previous chapters, how close proximity stimulates our sensory and nervous systems literally to work in sync and there are many different ways you can help to relax a brain and body beyond just cuddling or rhythmic rocking. Relaxing activities or strategies help to restore homeostasis or equilibrium within the child and support them on their journey towards self-regulation as we explored in Chapter 5. We have also noted that a key aspect of supporting children to relax is the self-regulation of our own arousal levels in order to begin the act of co-regulation. Co-regulation helps to ensure that children's stress is recognised rather than suppressed, ignored or avoided (Bergomi et al., 2013). As we saw in earlier chapters, if our limbic system is in a relaxed state, we can concentrate on more advanced frontal lobe development, such as engaging in more *Play* and *Talk* activities with the child.

## Play

The *Play* activity is about our need for *playfulness* which can start early on with some simple face play – copying a baby's expressions or making faces – and then moving into more complex play activities, some of which we explored in Chapter 6. We also saw how research has clearly linked play not just to physical and emotional well-being, but also to cognitive growth (Fiorelli and Russ, 2012). The need for playful interactions has been highlighted by Schore (2001a) who notes that *play states* provide opportunities to experience positive emotions (or positive affects). This helps to create 'positively charged curiosity that fuels the burgeoning self's exploration of novel socioemotional and physical environments' (2001a: 21). Similarly, Trevarthen (2005) points out that the caregiver relationship is not simply about being a secure base and safe haven, but is also about being a *friend and playmate*.

## Talk

Cairns (2014) explains that when young children feel settled through their playful, connected relationships, their brains are receptive to learning through *Talk*, which helps to forge more conscious thinking processes in our brain, enabling us to make sense of our experiences and translate them into words. The *Talk* activity links closely to the wealth of evidence available regarding children's later academic achievement and the nature and amount of talk they experience in their earliest years (Hart and Risely, 1995). It also relates to the development and co-creation of shared understanding or *intersubjectivity* as it is known (Trevarthen and Aitken, 2001). It is not just about talking to the child but is about tuning in, listening, sharing experiences and promoting understanding. *Talk* of course does not just encompass actual words, but incorporates the wealth of ways that we can communicate with children – mimicking sounds, providing a running commentary, singing nursery rhymes and reading stories.

## Mindful Moment

Cairns advocates that the Five to Thrive approach is underpinned by a *mindful* approach based on the principles of mindfulness. Cairns (2014) considers that mindfulness is a key attribute of caregiving for developing infant mental health. We saw in the Introduction that mindfulness involves increasing your awareness in a given moment and paying attention, with greater clarity, to what might be happening. This may enable you to be more flexible and adaptable and to take more considered action in your work with children. This links to some research undertaken by Deogardi and Davis (2008) which showed how practitioners can develop more attuned relationships with children by paying more attention to what is happening. They termed these *highly elaborative responses*, where practitioners noticed more in-depth aspects of the child's play – such as their physical and social actions – and attempted to interpret what these actions might mean in relation to the child's internal cognitive and emotional state. In this respect, they displayed mind-mindedness.

Looking back at some of the content of this chapter, think about what adopting a mindful and mind-mindedness approach might entail in your practice.

# Putting Five to Thrive into practice

The case study that follows provides a helpful illustration of how Five to Thrive has been applied in practice and how it can promote health and well-being, not just in the child but in the caregiver.

## Case Study

### Five to Thrive

A family support worker (FSW) used Five to Thrive (FTT) to support a mother and six-month-old child. The mother did not feel bonded to the baby and was deeply anxious, displaying numerous symptoms of post-natal depression.

The FSW started by asking the mother to find a minute or so a day to do a mirroring exercise when the baby was calm by copying the baby's facial expressions. The following week, the mother told the FSW that she'd been doing it often during nappy changes and hadn't noticed how many different expressions the baby had. The FSW was able to help the mother begin to tune into the baby's cues and RESPOND more to the baby's needs from doing this simple activity.

Next, the FSW suggested that she do a mindfulness-based activity during her daily routine and the mother chose getting her baby dressed. At the next visit, she asked the mother to reflect what things she had noticed and the mother said she had once again noticed things that she hadn't noticed before, e.g. how the baby seemed to watch her hands as she was dressing her and so was beginning to ENGAGE more with her.

The FSW asked the mother what things she likes to do to relax and the mother said 'have a bath', so she suggested she bring baby into the bath and to relax with her. Although the mother found this initially awkward she managed to relax and afterwards sat cuddling on a chair. Gradually, the mother was able to think about how she could RELAX the baby when the baby was stressed.

For the last two activities, Play and Talk, the FSW suggested some simple activities like singing a nursery rhyme and reading a story after the relaxing activities. Over time, she felt the mother was much more able to tune into her baby and respond and engage appropriately which led to the mother to do more PLAY and TALK activities.

The FSW was impressed by the effectiveness and simplicity of the FTT framework. She felt that the first three activities were particularly important in helping the attachment relationship in relatively easy, bite-size steps. She commented how the mother also found them manageable. Thinking about the baby in terms of either needing to soothe or to stimulate helped the mother feel that this was something she could do, so it was empowering and lessened her anxiety and depressive symptoms.

# Concluding comments – sustainable health and well-being

Leading academics at Harvard University have noted that 'a vital and productive society with a prosperous and sustainable future is built on a foundation of healthy child development' (NSCDC, 2010: 1). Furthermore, the Stern Review (2007) identified that more sustainable modes of world development were no longer an option but a necessity. Such sustainable development comprises not just environmental conservation and economic prosperity, but social and personal health and well-being (UNESCO, 2005).

Indeed, it is now believed that sustainable development should be a measure of overall quality of life, with opportunities to lead a healthy life along with equal and fair access to the resources needed for a decent standard of living (Fien et al., 2009). However, research has identified that contemporary childhood experience is increasingly detrimental to healthy development (Layard and Dunn, 2009). Therefore, there is a strong impetus for us to establish a more sustainable future for our children.

Professionals and parents are the key to breaking inter-generational cycles of dysfunction and underachievement, and to empowering children to reach their full potential. The evidence acknowledges that a child's developing brain architecture is positively shaped by reciprocal and dynamic interactions, as well as well-being being promoted and sustained through nurturing environments and supportive relationships (Rees et al., 2010; Statham and Chase, 2010). The Children's Society (2012) notes that the quality of relationships between children and their families is ten times more powerful in explaining their perceived levels of well-being than specific family structures. Experiencing consistent, safe and secure relationships has been shown to help ameliorate adverse childhood experiences (Fisher et al., 2014), so all children must be given opportunities to share in empathetic and nurturing environments and experiences. Participation in meaningful activities generates opportunities of satisfaction as a significant contributor and so improves well-being, self-esteem and mental health (Boyden and Dercon, 2012). Such intervention will benefit the individual immediately through increased quality of childhood experience and in the future through the development of knowledge and skill capacity for parenting. Learning through supportive and empathic living promotes inter-generational nurturing and well-being, thereby reducing the risk of future mental health problems and helping to break the vicious cycle of deprivation (DoH, 2011b).

In order to create a sustainable future, which includes breaking these inter-generational cycles of dysfunction, underachievement and unequal access to human, social and economic capital, early years professionals need a clear understanding of how to build children's social and emotional capability (NICE, 2012; Obrist et al., 2010). Success is now believed to be as much to do with socio-emotional and self-regulatory capacities as academic skills and knowledge (Heckman et al., 2006). Moreover, society must be value-centred, with a foundational focus on caring for and respecting human dignity and our universal rights (Kjørholt, 2013). As Perry states, 'what is most needed is a society that is safe, predictable, relational, enriched, and humane' in order to establish optimal health and well-being (2006: 28).

This book has shown that ensuring our practice rests on a psychoneurobiological perspective and bioecological model of human development, we can develop an enriched and attuned interpersonal environment which helps to lay the foundations for optimal health and well-being. In doing so, the book has highlighted some *growth-facilitating* strategies (Schore, 2001a) that can positively affect the brain, body and mind for sustainable health and well-being:

- firstly, to establish a safe, stable and responsive relational context that generates consistent and attuned interactions with adults to enhance children's learning and development, and nurtures an effective self-regulating stress response system;
- secondly, to create a co-constructed, balanced and enabling environment which promotes active exploration to generate resilience and learning power, and includes the provision of sound and appropriate nutrition.

Such practice will provide children with firm roots from which their engagement with life-long health and well-being can grow, empowering their own, their community's and future generations' health and well-being.

---

## Key Points

- Five to Thrive is an effective framework that can support practitioners' work with children and families.
- Finding a delicate balance between the *see-saw* of soothing and stimulating experiences and knowing *when and how* to initiate, sustain and/or terminate a soothing or stimulating activity is a pivotal part of the caregiver/practitioner's practice.
- Early years practitioners play an important role in breaking inter-generational cycles of deprivation and dysfunction by empowering young children and their families to take ownership of their health and well-being.
- An enriched, attuned, interpersonal, co-constructed, balanced and enabling environment lays the foundation for sustainable health and well-being.

---

# Useful Further Reading and Websites

- Siegel, D. and Bryson, T. (2011) *The Whole Brain Child: 12 Revolutionary Strategies to Nurture Your Child's Developing Mind.* New York: Random House. This book provides an accessible insight into the neuroscience that underpins the Five to Thrive approach.

- Music, G. (2011) *Nurturing Natures: Attachment and Children's Emotional, Sociocultural and Brain Development.* Hove: Psychology Press. This book provides a helpful insight into the processes that underlie sustainable health and well-being.
- Davis, J. (ed.) (2014) *Young Children and the Environment: Early Education for Sustainability.* Melbourne: Cambridge University Press. This book offers a detailed overview of sustainability in the early years including health and well-being.
- Further information about Five to Thrive can be found on the Kate Cairns Associates website at: http://www.katecairns.com/.

# REFERENCES

Action for Children (2014) *Child neglect: the scandal that never breaks.* Watford. Available at: http://www.actionforchildren.org.uk/policy-research/publications-and-briefings (Accessed 12 December 2014).

Ainsworth, M. (1979) 'Infant–mother attachment', *American Psychologist*, 34, pp.932–937.

Ainsworth, M., Blehar, M., Waters, E. and Wall, S. (1978) *Patterns of Attachment.* Hillsdale, NJ: Earlbaum.

Ainsworth, M., and Bowlby, J. (1991) 'An ethological approach to personality development', *American Psychological Association*, 46, pp.333–341.

Albon, D. and Mukherji, P. (2008) *Food and Health in Early Childhood.* London: Sage.

Allen, G. (2011) *Early intervention: the next steps.* Available at: http://www.dwp.gov.uk/early-intervention-next-steps.pdf (Accessed 3 March 2013).

Applegate, J. and Shapiro, J. (2005) *Neurobiology for Clinical Social Work: Theory and Practice.* New York: W. W. Norton and Company.

Arnold, C. and the Pen Green Team (2010) *Understanding Schemas and Emotion in Early Childhood.* London: Sage.

Ayres, A. (1972) *Sensory Integration and Learning Disorders.* Los Angeles: Western Psychological Services.

Badenoch, B. (2008) *Being a Brain-Wise Therapist, a Practical Guide to Interpersonal Neurobiology.* New York: W.W Norton and Company.

Balbernie, R. (2001) 'Circuits and circumstances: the neurobiological consequences of early relationship experiences and how they shape later behaviour', *Journal of Child Psychotherapy*, 27(3), pp. 237–255.

Balbernie, R. (2007) 'The move to intersubjectivity, a clinical and conceptual shift of perspective', *Journal of Child Psychotherapy*, 33(3), pp.308–324.

Ball, M., Moselle, K. and Pedersen, S. (2007) *Father's Involvement as a Determinant of Child Health.* Available at: http://www.fira.ca/cms/documents/122/PH_FI_Final_Full_Report.pdf (Accessed 11 January 2015).

Bandura, A. (1977) *Social Learning Theory.* Englewood Cliffs: Prentice-Hall.

Ben-Arieh, A. (2007) *Measuring and monitoring the well-being of young children around the world*. Available at: http://en.unesco.org/ (Accessed 4 December 2013).

Behen, M., Helder, E., Rothermel, R., Solomon, K. and Chugani, H. (2008) 'Incidence of specific absolute neurocognitive impairment in globally intact children with histories of early deprivation', *Child Neuropsychology*, 14 (5). pp.453–469.

Berger, K. (2011) *The Developing Person Through the Lifespan*. New York: Worth.

Bergin, C. and Bergin, D. (2009) 'Attachment in the Classroom', *Educational Psychology Review*, 21, pp.141–170.

Berk, L. (2003) *Child Development*. Boston: Pearson Education.

Benard, B. (1995) *Fostering Resilience in Children*. Available at: http://resilnet. uiuc.edu/library/benard95.html (Accessed 6 June 2014).

Bergomi, C., Ströhle, G., Michalak, J., Funke, F. and Berking, M. (2013) 'Facing the dreaded: does mindfulness facilitate coping with distressing experiences? A moderator analysis', *Cognitive Behaviour Therapy*, 42(1), pp.21–30.

Bion, W. (1967) *A Theory of Thinking in Second Thoughts*. London: Karnac.

Blackman, J. (2002) 'Early Intervention: A Global Perspective', *Infant and Young Children*, 15(2), pp.11–19.

Blakemore, S-J. and Frith, U. (2005) *The Learning Brain: Lessons for Education*. Oxford: Blackwell.

Blase, J. and Blase, J. (2004) *Handbook of Instructional Leadership*. London: Sage.

BDA (British Dietetic Association) (2013) *Diet, behaviour and learning in children*. Available at: https://www.bda.uk.com/foodfacts/home (Accessed 24 January 2015).

BDA (British Dietetic Association) (2014) *Healthy eating for children*. Available at https://www.bda.uk.com/foodfacts/home (Accessed 24 January 2015).

BNF (British Nutrition Foundation) (2014) *What not to eat when pregnant*. Available at: http://www.nutrition.org.uk/healthyliving/healthyeating (Accessed 2 January 2015).

BMA (British Medical Association) (2007) *Fetal alcohol spectrum disorder, a guide for healthcare professionals*. Available at: http://www.google.co.uk/url?sa=t&rct=j&q=&esrc=s&source=web&cd=2&ved=0CC0QFjAB&url=http%3A%2F%2Ffasaware.co.uk%2Fwp-content%2Fuploads%2F2014%2F10%2FFetalAlcoholSpectrumDisorders_tcm41-158035.pdf&ei=WNipVMKvC8GAU97-gcAD&usg=AFQjCNEWmpKylo8EgGJmF_bV6srXoDRXdA (Accessed 04 June 2014).

Bodrova, E. and Leong, D. (2011) Revisiting Vygtoskian perspectives on play and pedagogy, in Rogers, S. *Rethinking Play and Pedagogy in Early Childhood Contexts*. Abingdon: Routledge, pp. 60–72.

Boreham, C. and Riddoch, C. (2001) 'The physical activity, fitness and health of children', *Journal of Sports Science*, 19, pp.915–929.

Bowlby, J. (1969). *Attachment and Loss: Attachment, Vol. 1*. New York: Basic Books.

Bowlby, J. (1988) *A Secure Base: Clinical applications of attachment theory*. London: Routledge.

Boyden, J. and Dercon, S. (2012) *Child Development and Economic Development: Lessons and Future Challenges*. Available at: https://www.younglives.org.uk (Accessed: 12 December 2014).

Bradford, B. (2012) 'Policing and social identity, procedural justice, inclusion and cooperation between police and public', *Policing and Society*, 24(1) pp.22–43.

Bronfenbrenner, U. (2005) *Making Human Beings Human: Bioecological Perspectives on Human Development*. London: Sage.

Cairns, K. (2001) The effects of trauma on childhood learning, in Jackson, S. (ed.) *Nobody Ever Told Us School Matters*. London; BAAF, pp.191–205.

Cairns, K. (2014) *Five to Thrive: Five things you do every day that help your child's growing brain*. Dursley: KCA.

C4EO (Centre for Excellence in Outcomes) (2010) *Grasping the nettle: early intervention for children, families and communities*. Available at: https://www.family-action.org.uk/wp-content/uploads/2014/06/early_intervention_grasping_the_nettle_full_report.pdf (Accessed 11 December 2014).

Cancer Research UK (2014) *Bowel Cancer*. Available at: http://www.cancerresearchuk.org (Accessed: 31 December 2014).

Carlson, N. (2007) *Physiology of Behaviour*. Harlow: Pearson Education Ltd.

Carter, R. (2010) *Mapping the Mind*. London: Phoenix Press.

Child Welfare Information Gateway (2009) *Understanding the Effects of Maltreatment on Brain Development*. Available at: www.childwelfare.gov/pubs/issue_briefs/brain_development/ (Accessed 4 October 2013).

Cherniack, P. (2012) 'Vitamin D, Energy Regulation and Mental Health', in Riby, L., Smith, M. and Foster, J. (eds) *Nutrition and Mental Performance: A Lifespan Perspective*. Basingstoke: Palgrave Macmillan, pp.83–98.

Clarke, L., Ungerer, J., Chahoud, K., Johnson, S., and Stiefel, I. (2002) 'Attention deficit hyperactivity disorder is associated with attachment insecurity', *Clinical Child Psychology and Psychiatry*, 7(2), pp.179–98.

Claxton, G. (1999) *Wise Up: The Challenge of Lifelong Learning*: London: Bloomsbury.

Claxton, G. (2002) *Building Learning Power*: Bristol, TLO Ltd.

Codrington, R. (2010) A Family Therapist's look into Interpersonal Neurobiology and the adolescent brain: An interview with Dr Daniel Siegel. *The Australian and New Zealand Journal of Family Therapy*, 31 (3), pp. 285–299.

Cohen, J. and Stewart, I. (1995) *The Collapse of Chaos: Discovering Simplicity in a Complex World*. London: Penguin.

Commodari, E. (2013) 'Preschool teacher attachment, school readiness and risk of learning difficulties', *Early Childhood Research Quarterly*, 28, pp.123–133.

Conner, M. and Armitage, C. (2002). *The Social Psychology of Food*. Buckingham: Open University Press.

Cottrell, S. (2013) *The Study Skills Handbook*. London: Palgrave Macmillan.

Cozolino, L. (2013) The social neuroscience of Education. New York: WW Norton & Company

Cozolino, L. (2014) *The Neuroscience of Human Relationships*. New York: W.W. Norton and Co.

Damasio, A.R. (1994) *Descartes' Error: Emotion, Reason and the Human Brain*. New York: Grosset/Putnam.

Damasio, A.R. (1998) 'Emotion in the perspective of an integrated nervous system', *Brain Research Reviews*, 26, pp.83–86.

Davidson, R. and Begley, S. (2012) *The Emotional Life of Your Brain*. London: Hodder and Stoughton.

Deakin Crick, R., Broadfoot, P. and Claxton, G. (2004). 'Developing an Effective Lifelong Learning Inventory: the ELLI Project', *Assessment in Education*, 11 (3), pp.247–72.

Deakin Crick, R. (2006) *Learning Power in Practice*. London: Paul Chapman Publishing.

Deogardi, S. and Davis, B. (2008) 'Understanding infants: characteristics of early childhood practitioners' interpretations of infants and their behaviours', *Early Years*, 28(3), pp.221–34.

DfE (2011) *Parenting Early Intervention Programmes*. Research Report DFE-RR121(a). Available at:https://www.gov.uk/government/uploads/system/uploads/attachment_data/file/182715/DFE-RR121A.pdf (Accessed 12 January 2015).

DfE (Department for Education) (2013) *Sure Start Children's Centres Statutory Guidance*. Available at: https://www.gov.uk/government/uploads/system/uploads/attachment_data/file/273768/childrens_centre_stat_guidance_april_2013.pdf (Accessed 1 December 2014).

DfE (2014a) *Statutory Framework for the Early Years Foundation Stage*. London: DfE Publications.

DfE (2014b) *Mental health and behaviour in schools, DFE-00435-2014*. Available at: https://www.google.co.uk/?gws_rd=ssl#q=mental+health+and+behaviour+in+schools (Accessed 10 November 2014).

Diamond, L., Fagundes, C. and Butterworth, M. (2011) 'Attachment style, vagal tone and empathy during mother–adolescent interactions', *Journal of Research on Adolescence*, 22(1), pp.165–184.

DoH (Department of Health) (2009) *Healthy child programme, pregnancy and the first five years of life*. Available at: https://www.gov.uk/government/publications/healthy-child-programme-pregnancy-and-the-first-5-years-of-life (Accessed 20 August 2014).

DoH (2011a) *Healthy lives, healthy people: a call to action on obesity in England*. Available at: https://www.gov.uk/government/publications/healthy-lives-healthy-people-a-call-to-action-on-obesity-in-england (Accessed 7 January 2015).

DoH (2011b) *No health without mental health: a cross-government mental health outcomes strategy for people of all ages, DoH 14679*. Available at: https://www.gov.uk/government/publications/the-mental-health-strategy-for-england (Accessed 2 November 2014).

DoH (2012) *The Family Nurse Partnership Programme*. Available at: https://www.gov.uk/government/uploads/system/uploads/attachment_data/file/216864/The-Family-Nurse-Partnership-Programme-Information-leaflet.pdf (Accessed 22 December 2014).

DoH/NHS (Department of Health and the National Health Service) (2013) *The National Health Visitor Plan: Progress to date and implementation 2013 onwards.* Available at: http://www.england.nhs.uk/wp-content/uploads/2013/06/nati-hlth-vis-pln.pdf (Accessed 4 December 2014).

Domellöf, M. and Szymlek-Gay, E. (2012) 'Iron nutrition and neurodevelopment in young children', in Riby, L., Smith, M. and Foster, J. (eds) *Nutrition and Mental Performance: A Lifespan Perspective.* Basingstoke: Palgrave Macmillan, pp.13–28.

Donaldson, M. (1978) *Children's Minds.* London: Fontana Press.

Dovey. T.M. (2010) *Eating Behaviour.* Maidenhead: Open University Press.

Dwyer, J., Needham, L., Randall Simpson, J. and Shaver Heener, E. (2008) 'Parents report intrapersonal, interpersonal and environmental barriers to support healthy eating and physical activity among their pre-schoolers', *Applied Physiology, Nutrition and Metabolism,* 33(2), pp.338–346.

Early Education (2012) *Development Matters in the Early Years Foundation Stage (EYFS).* Available at: https://www.earlyeducation.org.uk/sites/default/files/Development%20Matters%20in%20the%20Early%20Years%20Foundation%20Stage%20-%20FINAL.pdf (Accessed 29 December 2014).

Edmonds, C. (2012) 'Water, Hydration Status and Cognitive Performance' in Riby, L., Smith, M. and Foster, J. (eds.) *Nutrition and Mental Performance: A Lifespan Perspective.* Basingstoke: Palgrave Macmillan, pp.193–211.

Eisenberg, N., and Fabes, R. (1995) 'The relation of young children's vicarious emotional responding to social competence, regulation, and emotionality', *Cognition & Emotion,* 9, pp.203–228.

Ellis, S. and Tod, J. (2009) *Behaviour for Learning: Proactive approaches to behaviour management.* Abingdon: Routledge.

Entwistle, F. (2013) The evidence and rationale for the UNICEF UK Baby Friendly Initiative standards. London: UNICEF UK.

Evans, G., Brooks-Gunn, J. and Klebanov, P. (2011) 'Stressing out the poor, chronic physiological stress and the income-achievement gap', *Pathways,* Winter 11, pp.16–21.

Feldman, R. (2007) 'Parent–Infant Synchrony: Biological foundations and developmental outcomes', *Current Directions in Psychological Science,* 16(6), pp.340–45.

Feldman, R. and Eidelman, A (2009) 'Biological and environmental initial conditions shape the trajectories of cognitive and socio-emotional development across the first years of life', *Developmental Science,* 12(1), pp.194–200.

Feldman, R., Greenbaum, C. and Yirmiya, N. (1999) 'Mother–infant affect synchrony as an antecedent of the emergence of self-control', *Developmental Psychology,* 35, pp.223–231.

Feldman, R., Magori-Cohence, R., Galili, G., Singer, M and Louzounc, Y. (2011) 'Mother and infant coordinate heart rhythms through episodes of interaction synchrony', *Infant Behavior and Development,* 34, pp.569–577.

ffield, M. (2014) 'Active Learning in the Early Years' in Vickery, A. (eds.) *Developing Active Learning in the Primary Classroom.* London: Sage, pp.19–38.

Fien, J., Maclean, R. and Park, M. (Eds) (2009) *Work, Learning and Sustainable Development: Opportunities and Challenges.* Dordrecht: Springer.

Fiorelli, J. and Russ, S. (2012) 'Pretend play, coping, and subjective well-being in children: A follow-up study', *American Journal of Play,* 5 (1), pp.81–103.

Fisher, B., Hanson, A. and Raden, T. (2014) *Start early to build a healthy future: the research linking early learning and health.* Available at: http://www.the ounce.org/start-early-to-build-a-healthy-future (Accessed 2 April 2014).

Fivush, R. (2006) 'Scripting attachment: Generalized event representations and internal working models', *Attachment and Human Development,* 8, pp.283–289.

Fleer, M. (2005) 'Developmental fossils – unearthing the artefacts of early childhood education: The reification of child development', *Australian Journal of Early Childhood,* 30(2), pp.2–7.

Fonagy, P., Gergely, G., Jurist, E. and Target, M. (2004) *Affect Regulation, Mentalization and the Development of the Self.* London: Karnac.

Forest Schools (2015) *Forest schools education.* Available at: www.forestschools.com (Accessed 10 January 2015).

Gandy, J. (2012) 'First findings of the United Kingdom Fluid Intake Study'. *Nutrition Today.* 47(4), pp.S1–S37.

Geake, J. (2009) *The Brain at School: Educational Neuroscience in the Classroom.* Maidenhead: Open University and Mc Graw Hill.

Geddes, H. (2006) *Attachment in the Classroom: The links between children's early experience, emotional wellbeing and performance in school.* London: Worth Publishing.

Gerhardt, S. (2004) *Why Love Matters: How affection shapes a baby's brain.* London: Routledge.

Ghate, D., Coe, C. and Lewis, J. (2013) *My Baby's Brain in Hertfordshire: The independent evaluation of Phase Two 2012 to 2013.* The Colebrooke Centre for Evidence and Implementation and Warwick Medical School, University of Warwick. Available at: http://www.cevi.org.uk/docs2/My_Baby%27s_Brain_final_report_February_2014.pdf (Accessed 31 December 2014).

Gilbert, L., Rose, J. and McGuire-Snieckus, R. (2014) 'Promoting children's wellbeing and sustainable citizenship through emotion coaching' in Thomas, M. (ed.) *A Child's World: Working together for a better future.* Aberystwyth: Aberystwyth Press.

Glaser, D. (2000) 'Child abuse and neglect and the brain: A Review', *Journal of Child Psychology and Psychiatry,* 41(1), pp.97–116.

Goddard-Blythe, S. (2008) *What Babies and Children Really Need.* Stroud: Hawthorne Press.

Goleman, D. (1995) *Emotional Intelligence.* New York: Bantam Books.

Gopnik, A., Meltzoff, A. and Kuhl, P. (1999) *How Babies Think.* London: Weidenfeld & Nicholson.

Gottman, J. (1994) *What Predicts Divorce? The Relationship between Marital Processes and Marital Outcomes.* New Jersey: Lawrence Erlbaum.

Gottman, J. and DeClaire, J. (1997) *The Heart of Parenting: Raising an Emotionally Intelligent Child.* New York: Simon and Schuster paperbacks.

Gottman, J., Katz, L. and Hooven, C. (1997) *Meta-emotion: How families communicate emotionally.* New York: Psychology Press.

Greenfield, S. (2002) 'Mind, brain and consciousness', *British Journal of Psychiatry*, 181, pp.91–93.

Gross, J. (2013) 'Emotion regulation: taking stock and moving forward', *American Psychological Association*, 13(3), pp.359–365.

Grotberg (1995) *The International Resilience Project.* Available at http://resilnet. uiuc.edu/library/grotb97a.html (Accessed 9 November 2014).

Gunnar, M. and Donzellas, B. (2002) 'Social regulation of the cortisol levels in early human development', *Psychoneuroendocrinology*, 1–2, pp.199–220.

Gunnar, M. and Quevedo, K. (2007) 'The neurobiology of stress and development', *Annual Review of Psychology*, 58, pp.145–73.

Gus, L., Rose, J., Gilbert, L. (2015) 'Emotion Coaching: a universal strategy for supporting and promoting sustainable emotional and behavioural well-being'. *Journal of Educational and Child Psychology*, 32(1), pp 31–41.

Guy, C. and Burghart, A. (2014) *Breakthrough Britain 2015: An overview.* Available at: http://www.centreforsocialjustice.org.uk/publications/breakthrough-britain-2015-an-overview (Accessed 15 November 2014).

Haddon, A., Goodman, H., Park, J. and Deakin Crick, R. (2005) 'Evaluating Emotional Literacy in Schools: The Development of the School Emotional Environment for Learning Survey', *Pastoral Care in Education: An International Journal of Personal, Social and Emotional Development*, 23(4), pp.5–16.

Halpenny, A. and Pettersen, J. (2014) *Introducing Piaget: A guide for practitioners and students in early years education.* Abingdon: Routledge.

Ham, J., and Tronick, E. (2006). 'Infant resilience to the stress of the still-face: Infant and maternal psychophysiology are related', *Annals of the New York Academy of Sciences*, 1094, pp.297–302.

Hands, B., Martin, M. and Lynch, P. (2004) *Fundamental movement skills, Book 1: Learning, teaching and assessment.* Perth: Western Australia Ministry for Education.

Hark, L. and Deen D. (2005) *Nutrition for Life.* London: Dorling Kindersley.

Harkness, S., Gregg, P. and MacMillan, L. (2012) *Poverty: the role of institutions, behaviours and culture.* Available at: www.jrf.org.uk/publications (Accessed 15 November 2014).

Hart, B. and Risley, T. (1995) *Meaningful Differences in the Everyday Experience of Young American Children.* Baltimore: Brookes Publishing.

Hasselhölt, S., Tveden-Nyborg, P. and Lykkesfeldt, J. (2012) 'Vitamin C and its role in brain development and cognition', in Riby, L., Smith, M. and Foster, J. (eds) *Nutrition and Mental Performance: A Lifespan Perspective.* Basingstoke: Palgrave Macmillan, pp.29–52.

Havighurst, S., Wilson, K., Harley, A. and Prior, M. (2009) 'Tuning in to kids: An emotion-focused parenting program – initial findings from a community trial', *Journal of Community Psychology*, 37(8), pp.1008–1023.

Heckman, J. (2011) 'The economics of inequality: The value of early childhood education', *American Educator*, 35(1), pp.31–35, 47.

Heckman, J., Stixrud, J. and Urzua, S. (2006) 'The effects of cognitive and non-cognitive abilities on labor market outcomes and social behaviour', *Journal of Labor Economics,* 24(3), pp.411–482.

Hill, J. and Peters, J. (1998) 'Environmental contributions to the obesity epidemic', *Science,* 280 (5368): 1371–4.

Hornor, G. (2008) 'Reactive attachment disorder', *Journal of Pediatric Health Care,* 22.4, 234–39.

Horton, R. 2003 'The neglect of child neglect', *The Lancet,* 361, p.443.

Howard-Jones, P. (2014a) 'Neuroscience and education: myths and messages', *Nature Reviews Neuroscience,* 15(12), pp.817–814.

Howard-Jones, P. (2014b) 'Evolutionary perspectives on mind, brain and education', *Mind, Brain, and Education,* 8(1), pp. 21–33.

Howe, D. (2011) *Attachment Across the Lifecourse: A Brief Introduction.* London: Palgrave Macmillan.

Hutchings, M. (2008) 'The Ecology of Learning', in Ward, S., *Education Studies: A Student's Guide.* London: Routledge, pp.223–237.

Immordino-Yang, M. (2011) 'Implications of affective and social neuroscience for educational theory', *Educational Philosophy and Theory,* 43(1), pp. 98–103.

IRDG (Integrated Review Development Group) (2013) *The Integrated Review: Update on progress.* Available at: http://www.4children.org.uk/Files/ba82693e-9279-4db8-9a94-a1cd00b92cc8/Sue-Robb---CC-Integrated-Review-May-13---to-show-if-there-is-time.pdf (Accessed 16 December 2014).

Izard, C. (1982) *Measuring Emotions in Infants and Children.* Cambridge: Cambridge University Press.

Jefferson-Buchanan, R. (2011) 'The Fundamental Movement Skills Programme: Physical Development Challenges and Opportunities in the Primary School Context', in Howe, A. and Richards, V. (eds.) *Bridging the transition from primary to Secondary School.* Abingdon: Routledge, pp. 113–126.

Kabat-Zinn, J. (2006) 'Mindfulness-based interventions in context: Past, present, and future', *Clinical Psychology: Science and Practice,* 10, pp.144–156.

Keenan, T. and Evans, S. (2009) *An Introduction to Child Development.* London: Sage.

Kjørholt, A. (2013) 'Childhood as social investment, rights and the valuing of education', *Children and Society,* 27, pp.245–257.

Knight, S. (2013) *Forest School and Outdoor Learning in the Early Years.* London: Sage.

Kok, B., Coffey, K., Cohn, M., Catalino, L., Vacharkulksemsuk, T., Algoe, S., Brantley, M. and Fredrickson, B. (2013) 'How positive emotions build physical health: perceived social connections account for the upward spiral between positive emotions and vagal tone', *Association for Psychological Science,* 24 (7), pp.1123–1132.

Laevers, F. (1994) *Defining and Assessing Quality in Early Childhood Education.* Leuven: Leuven University Press.

Larkin, M. (2013) *Health and Well-Being Across the Life Course.* London: Sage.

Lawrence, D. (2006) *Enhancing Self-esteem in the Classroom.* London: Paul Chapman.

Layard, R. and Dunn, J. (2009) *A Good Childhood: Searching for Values in a Competitive Age*. London: Penguin.

Lean, M. (2006) *Fox and Cameron's Food Science, Nutrition and Health*. London: Hodder Arnold.

Leibermann, H. (2007) 'Hydration and cognition: a critical review and recommendations for future research', *Journal of the American College of Nutrition*, 26(5), pp.555S–561S.

Le Page, J-F. and Theoret H. (2007) 'The mirror neuron system, grasping others' actions from birth', *Developmental Science*, 10(5), pp.513–523.

Lemche, E., Giampietro, V., Surguladze, S., Amaro, E., Andrew, C., Williams, S., Brammer, M., Lawrence, N., Maier, M., Russell, T., Simmons, A., Ecker, C., Joraschky, P. and Phillips, M. (2006) 'Human attachment security is mediated by the amygdala: Evidence from combined fMRI and psychophysiological measures', *Human Brain Mapping*, 27(8), pp.623–635.

Lewkowicz, D. (2011) 'The biological implausibility of the nature-nurture dichotomy and what it means for the study of infancy', *Infancy*, 16(4), pp.331–367.

MacInnes, T., Aldridge, H., Bushe, S., Tinson, A. and Barry Born, T. (2014) *Monitoring poverty and social exclusion 2014*. [Online]. Available at: http://www.jrf.org.uk/publications/monitoring-poverty-and-social-exclusion-2014 (Accessed 12 December 2014).

Macintyre, C. (2012) *Enhancing Learning Through Play: A developmental perspective for early years settings*. Abingdon: Routledge.

Maclean, P. (1990) *The Triune Brain*. New York: Plenum Press.

Manning-Morton, J. (ed.) (2014) *Exploring Well-being in the Early Years*. Maidenhead: Open University Press.

Manning-Morton and Thorp, M. (2003) *Key times for play: The first three years* (debating play). Maidenhead: Open University Press

Mansfield, D. and Doutre, G. (2011) 'Food for thought: children's view on the psychological aspect of childhood obesity', *Educational and Child Psychology*, 28(4), pp.23–36.

Marmot, M. (2010) *Fair Society, Healthy Lives*. Available at: http://www.instituteofhealthequity.org/projects/fair-society-healthy-lives-the-marmot-review (Accessed 23 March 2011).

Maslow, A. (1954) *Motivation and Personality*. New York: Harper.

Matthews, B. (2006) *Engaging Education: Developing Emotional Literacy, Equity and Co-education*. Berkshire: Open University Press.

McCaffrey, T and Livingstone, B. (2009) 'Childhood Origins of Adult Obesity', *Nutrition in Practice*, 10, (1), pp.1–3.

McCrory, E., De Brito, S. and Viding, E. (2010) 'Research Review, the neurobiology and genetics of maltreatment and adversity', *Journal of Child Psychology and Psychiatry*, 51(10), pp.1079–1095.

McNamee, A., Mercurio, M. and Peloso, J. (2007) 'Who cares about caring in early childhood teacher education programs', *Journal of Early Childhood Teacher Education*, 28, pp. 277–88.

McSherry, D. (2011) 'Lest we forget, remembering the consequences of child neglect, a clarion call to feisty advocates', *Child Care in Practice*, 17(2), pp.103–113.

Meins, E. (1999) 'Sensitivity, security and internal working models: bridging the transmission gap', *Attachment and Human Development*, 1(3), pp.325–42.

Melhuish, E. (2014) 'The Impact of Early Childhood Education and Care on Improved Wellbeing', in British Academy Report *If you could do one thing...Nine local actions to reduce health inequalities*. pp. 33–43. Available at: http://www.britac.ac.uk/policy/Health_Inequalities.cfm (Accessed 14 December 2014).

Meins, E. Fernyhough, C., Fradley, E. and Tuckey, M. (2001) 'Rethinking maternal sensitivity: Mothers' comments on infants' mental processes predict security of attachment at 12 months', *Journal of Child Psychology and Psychiatry*, 42(5), pp.637–648.

Moore, G., and Calkins, S. (2004) 'Infants' vagal regulation in the still-face paradigm is related to dyadic coordination of mother–infant interaction', *Developmental Psychology*, 40, pp.1068–1080.

Moss, S. (2012) *Natural Childhood*. National Trust. Available at: http://www.nationaltrust.org.uk/document-1355766991839/ (Accessed 2 January 2014).

Moss, E. and St-Laurent, D. (2001) 'Attachment at school age and academic performance', *Developmental Psychology*, 37(6), pp.863–874.

Moylett, H. (2013) 'How young children learn: introduction and overview', in Moylett, H. (ed.) *Characteristics of Effective Early Learning*. Maidenhead: Open University Press, pp.1–14.

Moyles, J. (ed.) (2015) *The Excellence of Play*. Maidenhead: Open University Press.

Music, G. (2011) *Nurturing Natures: Attachment and children's emotional, socio-cultural and brain development*. Hove: Psychology Press.

NCB (National Children's Bureau) (2012) *A know how guide: The EYFS progress check at age two*. Available at: https://www.gov.uk/government/uploads/system/uploads/attachment_data/file/175311/EYFS_-_know_how_materials.pdf (Accessed 29 November 2014).

Nelson, C., Bos, K., Gunnar, M. and Sonuga-Barke, E. (2011) 'The neurobiological toll of early human deprivation', *Monographs of the Society for Research in Child Development*, 76(4), pp.127–146.

NHS (National Health Service) (2014a) *Start4Life*. Available at: http://www.nhs.uk/start4life/Pages/pregnancy-health-tips.aspx (Accessed: 13 December 2014).

NHS National Health Service (2014b) *Eat Well Plate*. Available at: http://www.nhs.uk/Livewell/Goodfood/Pages/eatwell-plate.aspx. (Accessed 31 December 2014).

NHS (National Health Service) (2015a) *The MMR vaccine*. Available at: http://www.nhs.uk/Conditions/vaccinations/Pages/mmr-vaccine.aspx (Accessed 7 January 2015).

NHS (2015b) *Pregnancy and having a baby*. Available at: http://www.nhs.uk/Conditions/pregnancy-and-baby (Accessed 8 January 2015).

NICE (National Institute for Health and Care Excellence) (2009) *Promoting mental wellbeing at work*. NICE public health guidance 22. Available at: https://www.nice.org.uk/guidance/ph22/resources/guidance-promoting-mental-wellbeing-at-work-pdf (Accessed 21 June 2015).

NICE (National Institute for Health and Care Excellence) (2012) *Social and emotional wellbeing: early years.* Available at: http://www.nice.org.uk/guidance/ph40 (Accessed 5 June 2014).

NIMH (National Institute of Mental Health) (2013) *Years of life lost among public mental health clients by state.* Available at: http://www.nimh.nih.gov/statistics/2YEARS_STATE.shtml (Accessed 27 December 2014).

NSCDC (National Scientific Council on the Developing Child) (2004) *Young Children Develop in an Environment of Relationships, working Paper, No. 1.* Available at: www.developingchild.harvard.edu (Accessed 22 December 2014).

NSCDC (2010) *The Foundations of Lifelong Health Are Built in Early Childhood.* Available at: http://www.developingchild.harvard.edu (Accessed 31 December 2014).

NSCDC (2012) *The Science of neglect: The persistence absence of responsive care disrupts the developing brain: working paper 12.* Available at: http://www.developingchild.harvard.edu (Accessed 10 October 2014).

NSCDC (2014). *Excessive Stress Disrupts the Architecture of the Developing Brain: Working Paper 3.* Available at: http://www.developingchild.harvard.edu (Accessed 15 September 2014).

NSPCC (National Society for the Prevention of Cruelty to Children) (2011) *All Babies Count: Prevention and protection for vulnerable babies.* Available at: http://www.nspcc.org.uk/globalassets/documents/research-reports/all-babies-count-prevention-protection-vulnerable-babies-report.pdf (Accessed 22 October 2014).

Obrist, B., Pfeiffer, C. and Henley, R. (2010) 'Multi-layered social resilience; a new approach to mitigation research', *Progress in Development Studies*, 10(4), pp.283–293.

O'Connor, M. and Russell, A. (2004) *Identifying the incidence of psychological trauma and post-trauma symptoms in children*, the Clackmannanshire Report. Clackmannanshire: Clackmannanshire Council Psychological Service.

Ogden, J. (2012) *Health Psychology: A Textbook.* Maidenhead Open University Press.

Olds, D., Kitzman, H., Cole, R. and Robinson, J. (1997) 'Theoretical foundations of a program of home visitation for pregnant women and parents of young children', *Journal of Psychology*, 2 (1), pp.9–25.

ONS (Office for National Statistics) (2014*) Children's Well-being.* Available at: http://www.ons.gov.uk/ons/rel/wellbeing/measuring-national-well-being/children-s-well-being--2014/rpt--- (Accessed 11 January 2015).

O'Sullivan, T. (2012) 'Exploring B Vitamins and their impact on cognitive function and mood from conception to early adulthood', in Riby, L., Smith M., and Foster, J. (eds) (2012) *Nutrition and Mental Performance: A Lifespan Perspective.* Basingstoke: Palgrave Macmillan, pp.53–82.

Panfile, T. and Laible, D. (2012) *Attachment Security and Child's Empathy: The mediating role of emotional regulation.* Merrill-Palmer Quarterly, 58 (1), pp.1–21.

Panksepp, J. (1998) *Affective Neuroscience.* New York: Oxford University Press.

Parker-Rees, R. (2010) 'Active playing and learning', in Parker-Rees, R., Leeson, C., Willan, J. and Savage, J. (eds) *Early Childhood Studies.* Exeter: Learning Matters.

Paterson, C. (2011) *Parenting Matters: Early years and social mobility.* Available at: http://www.centreforum.org/assets/pubs/parenting-matters.pdf (Accessed 2 December 2014).

Patterson, T., Rapsey, C. and Glue, P. (2013) 'Systematic review of cognitive development across childhood in Down syndrome, implications for treatment intervention', *Journal of Intellectual Disability Research,* 57(4), pp.306–318.

Perry, B. (2006) 'Applying principles of neurodevelopment to clinical work with maltreated and traumatised children: The neurosequential model of therapeutics', in Boyd, N. (ed.) *Working with Traumatised Youth in Child Welfare.* New York: Guilford Press, pp.27–52.

Perry, B. and Szlavitz, M. (2006) *The Boy Who was Raised as a Dog: And Other Stories from a Child Psychiatrist's Notebook. What traumatised children can teach us about loss, love and healing.* New York: Basic Books.

PHE (2014) Public Health England. Available at: http://www.noo.org.uk?NOO_about_obesity/child_obesity (Accessed 11th January 2015).

Piaget, J. (1954) *The Construction of Reality in the Child.* New York: Basic Books.

Piaget, J. (1978) *The Development of Thought.* Oxford: Blackwell.

Pollard, E. and Lee, P. (2002) 'Child Well-being: A systematic review of the literature', *Social Indicators Research,* 61, pp.59–78.

Pollock, N. (2009) 'Sensory integration: A review of the current state of the evidence', *Occupational Therapy Now,* 11(5), pp.5–10.

Porges, S. (2011) *The Polyvagal Theory: Neurophysiological Foundations of Emotions, Attachment, Communication, and Self-regulation.* New York: Norton and Company.

Rees, G., Bradshaw, J., Goswami, H., and Keung, A. (2010) *Understanding children's well-being: A national survey of young people's well-being.* London: The Children's Society.

Rees, G., Goswami, H. and Pople, L. (2013) *The Good Childhood Report 2013.* London: The Children's Society.

Richards, V. (2011a) 'Adolescent Development: Intellectual and Emotional Changes, in Howe, A. and Richards, V. (eds) *Bridging the Transition from Primary to Secondary School.* Abingdon: Routledge, pp.41–55.

Richards, V. (2011b) 'Adolescent Development: Personal and Social Changes', in Howe, A. and Richards, V. (eds) *Bridging the Transition from Primary to Secondary School.* Abingdon: Routledge, pp.56–70.

Ridley, M. (2004) *Nature via nurture.* New York: HarperCollins.

Rizzolatti, G. and Sinigaglia, C. (2010) 'The functional role of the parieto-frontal mirror circuit: interpretation and misinterpretations', *Nature Reviews Neuroscience,* 11, pp.264–274.

Roberts, R. (2006) *Self-Esteem and Early Learning: Key people from Birth to School.* London: Sage.

Roberts, R. (2010) *Wellbeing from Birth.* London: Sage.

Rogers, S. (2011) *Rethinking Play and Pedagogy in Early Childhood Contexts.* Abingdon: Routledge.

Rogers, S. and Evans, J. (2006) *Inside Role Play in Early Childhood Education.* London: Routledge.

Rogoff, B. (2003) *The Cultural Nature of Human Development.* Oxford: Oxford University Press.

Rose, J., Gilbert, L., McGuire-Snieckus, R. (2015) 'Emotion Coaching – a strategy for promoting behavioural self-regulation in children and young people in schools: A pilot study', *European Journal of Social and Behavioural Sciences,* 13(2), pp. 1766–1790.

Rose, J. and Rogers, S. (2012a) *The Role of the Adult in Early Years Settings.* Milton Keynes: Open University Press.

Rose, J. and Rogers, S. (2012b) 'Principles under pressure: Student teachers' perspectives on final teaching practice in early childhood classrooms', *International Journal of Early Years Education,* 20(1), p. 43–58.

Rose, N. and Abi-Rached, J. (2013) *Neuro: The New Brain Sciences and the Management of the Mind.* Oxford: Princeton University Press.

Rushton, S., Juola-Rushton, A. and Larkin, E. (2010) 'Neuroscience, play and early childhood education: connections, implications and assessment', *Early Childhood Education Journal,* 37, pp.351–361.

Rushton, S. (2011) 'Neuroscience, early childhood education and play: we are doing it right', *Early Childhood Education,* 39, pp.89–94.

Rutten, B., Hammels, C., Geschwind, N., Menne-Lothmann, C., Pishva, E., Schuers, K., Van Den Hove, D., Kenis, G., Van Os, J. and Wichers, M. (2013) 'Resilience in mental health: linking psychological and neurobiological perspectives', *Acta Psychiatricia Scandinavia,* 128, pp.3–20.

Sadates, R. and Dex, S. (2012) *Multiple risk factors in young children's development.* Available at: www.cls.ioe.ac.uk/shared/get-file.ashx?id=1327&item type=document (Accessed 4 December 2014).

Salovey, P. and Meyer, J. (1990) 'Emotional Intelligence', *Imagination, Cognition and Personality,* 9, pp.185–211.

Salovey, P., Rothman, A., Detweiler, J., and Steward, W. (2000) 'Emotional states and physical health', *American Psychologist,* 55, pp.110–121.

Sander, D. (2013) 'Models of Emotion: The affective neuroscience approach', in Armony, J. and Vuilleumier, P. (eds) *The Cambridge handbook of human affective neuroscience.* Cambridge: Cambridge University Press, pp.5–54.

Save the Children (2014) *The Child Poverty Act.* Available at: http://www.savethe children.org.uk/about-us/what-we-do/child-poverty/the-child-poverty-act (Accessed 24 November 2014).

Schaffer, R. (1996) *Social Development.* Oxford: Blackwell Publishing.

Schaffer, R. (2004) *Introducing Child Psychology.* Oxford: Blackwell Publishing.

Schaffer, R. and Emerson, P. (1964) 'The development of social attachments in infancy', *Monographs of the Society for Research in Child Development,* 29(3).

Schaverien, J. (2011) 'Boarding School Syndrome: Broken attachments, a hidden trauma', *British Journal of Psychotherapy*, 27(2), pp.138–155.

Schore, A. (1994) *Affect Regulation and the Origin of the Self: The Neurobiology of Emotional Development*. New Jersey: Lawrence Erlbaum.

Schore, A. (2001a) 'Effects of a secure attachment relationship on right brain development, affect regulation and infant mental health', *Infant Mental Health Journal*, 22(1–2), pp.7–66.

Schore, A. (2001b) 'The effects of early relational trauma on right brain development, affect regulation and infant mental health', *Infant Mental Health Journal*, Vol. 22(1–2), pp.201–269.

Schore, A. (2014) 'Early interpersonal neurobiological assessment of attachment and autistic spectrum disorders', *Frontiers in Psychology*, 5 (1049). Available at: http://journal.frontiersin.org/Journal/10.3389/fpsyg.2014.01049/full (Accessed 7 December 2014).

Schoffham, S. and Barnes, J. (2011) 'Happiness matters: towards a pedagogy of happiness and well-being', *The Curriculum Journal*, 22(4), pp.535–548.

Seligman, M. (2003) *Authentic Happiness*. New York: Basic Books.

Seligman, S. and Harrison, A. (2012) 'Infancy research, infant health, and adult psychotherapy; mutual influences', *Infant Mental Health Journal*, 33(4), pp.339–349.

Seung, S. (2012), *Connectome: How the brain's wiring makes us who we are*. New York: Houghton Mifflin Harcourt Publishing Company.

Shaffer, D. (1999) *Developmental Psychology: Childhood and Adolescence*. London: Brooks/Cole Publishing Company.

Shaughnessy, J. (2012) 'The challenge for English schools in responding to current debates on behaviour and violence', *Pastoral Care in Education: An International Journal of Personal, Social and Emotional Development*, 30(2), pp.87–97.

Shaw, S. (2010) *Parents, Children, Young People and the State*. Maidenhead: Open University Press/ McGraw-Hill Education.

Shetty, P. (2003) 'Malnutrition and Undernutrition', *Medecine*, 31(4), pp.18–32.

Shonkoff, J. (2010) 'Building a new biodevelopmental framework to guide the future of early childhood policy', *Child Development*, 81(1), pp.357–367.

Shonkoff, J. and Phillips, D. (2000) *From Neurons to Neighbourhoods: The Science of Early Child Development*. Washington: National Academy Press.

Shonkoff, J., Boyce, W. and McEwen, B. (2009) 'Neuroscience, molecular biology and the childhood roots of health disparities: Building a new framework for health promotion and disease prevention', *Journal of the American Medical Association*, 301(21), pp.2252–2259.

Shonkoff, J. and Garner, A. (2012) 'The lifelong effects of early Childhood Adversity and toxic stress', *American Academy of Pediatrics*, 129(1), pp.232–246.

Shonkoff, J., Richter, L., Van der Gaag, J. and Bhutta, Z. (2012) 'An integrated scientific framework for child survival and early childhood development', *Pediatrics*, 129(2), pp.460–472.

Schore, A.N. (1994) *Affect Regulation and the Origin of the Self: The Neurobiology of Emotional Development*. New Jersey: Lawrence Erlbaum.

Schore, A.N. (2001a) 'Effects of a secure attachment relationship on right brain development, affect regulation and infant mental health', *Infant Mental Health Journal,* 22 (1–2), pp.7–66.

Schore, A.N. (2001b) 'The effects of early relational trauma on right brain development, affect regulation and infant mental health', *Infant Mental Health Journal,* 22 (1–2), pp.201–269.

Schore, A.N. (2014) 'Early interpersonal neurobiological assessment of attachment and autistic spectrum disorders', *Frontiers in Psychology,* 5 (1049), pp.1–13.

Siegel, D. (1999) *Pocket Guide to Interpersonal Neurobiology.* New York: W.W. Norton and Company.

Siegel, D. (2006) 'An interpersonal neurobiology approach to psychotherapy', *Psychiatric Annals,* 36(4), pp.248–256.

Siegel, D. (2012) *The Developing Mind: How Relationships and the Brain Interact to Shape Who We Are.* New York: The Guilford Press.

Siegel, D. and Bryson, T. (2011) *The Whole Brain Child: 12 Revolutionary Strategies to Nurture Your Child's Developing Mind.* New York: Random House Publishers.

Siegler, R., DeLoache, J. Eisenburg, N. and Saffran, J. (2014) *How Children Develop.* New York: Worth.

Siraj-Blatchford, I., Sylva, K., Mattock, S., Gilden, R. and Bell, D. (2002) *Researching Effective Pedagogy in the Early Years (REPEY).* London: HMSO.

Siraj-Blatchford, I., Clarke, K. and Needham, M. (2007) *The Team Around the Child: Multi-agency Working in the Early Years.* Stoke on Trent: Trentham Books.

Skinner, B.F. (1974) *About Behviourism.* New York: Random House.

SMCPC (Social Mobility and Child Poverty Commission) (2014) *State of the Nation 2014: Social Mobility and Child Poverty in Great Britain.* Available at: www.gov.uk/government/publications (Accessed 27 November 2014).

Smith, P., Cowie, H. and Blades, M. (2011) *Understanding Children's Development.* Chichester: John Wiley and Sons.

Spiegal, B., Gill, T., Harbottle, H. and Ball, D. (2014) 'Children's play space and safety management: rethinking the role of play equipment standards', *Sage Open,* January-March, pp.1–11.

Spilt, J., Koomen, H. and Thijs, J. (2011) 'Teacher wellbeing: The importance of teacher–student relationships', *Educational Psychology Review,* 23, pp.457–477.

Sroufe, A. (1995) *Emotional Development.* Cambridge: Cambridge University Press.

Sroufe, A. and Siegel, D. (2011) *The Verdict Is In: The case for attachment theory.* Available at: http://www.drdansiegel.com/uploads/1271-the-verdict-is-in.pdf (Accessed 26 December 2014).

Statham, J. and Chase, E. (2010). *Childhood Wellbeing: A brief overview.* Loughborough: Childhood Wellbeing Research Centre.

Stern, D. (2002) *The First Relationship.* Cambridge, MA: Harvard University Press.

Stern, N. (2007) *The Economics of Climate Change: The Stern Review.* Cambridge: Cambridge University Press.

Stiglitz, J., Sen, A., and Fitoussi, J. (2010) *Report by the commission on the measurement of economic performance and social progress.* Paris: Commission on the Measurement of Economic Performance and Social Progress.

Straub, R. (2014) *Health Psychology a Biopsychosocial Approach,* 4th Edn. New York: Worth.

Sunderland, M. (2007) *What Every Parent Needs to Know: The incredible effects of love, nurture and play on your child's development.* London: Dorling Kindersley.

Taylor, M. (2011) 'In favour of life and wholeness', in New Economics Foundation, *The Practical Politics of Well-being,* pp.27–33. Available at: http://www.new economics.org/publications/entry/the-practical-politics-of-well-being (Accessed 10 January 2015).

The Children's Society (2012) *Promoting positive well-being for children: A report for decision makers in parliament, central government and local areas.* Available at: http://www.childrenssociety.org.uk/what-we-do/research/well-being/publications/promoting-positive-well-being-children (Accessed 15 January 2015).

Thomas, S. (2008) *Nurturing Babies and Children Under Four.* London: Pearson.

Tickell, C. (2011) *The Early Years: Foundations for Life Health and Learning.* London: Department for Education.

Tovey, (2007) *Playing Outdoors: Spaces and Places, Risks and Challenge.* Maidenhead: Open University Press.

Trevarthen, C. (2005) 'Stepping away from the mirror: Pride and shame in adventures in companionship. Reflections on the nature and emotional needs of infant intersubjectivity', in Carter, C., Ahnert, L., Grossmann, K., Hrdy, S., Lamb, M., Porges, S. and Sachser, N., (eds) *Attachment and Bonding: A New Synthesis,* Dahlem Workshop Report 92. Cambridge, MA: MIT Press.

Trevarthen, C. (2011a) 'What young children give to their learning, making education work to sustain a community and its culture', *European Early Childhood Education Research Journal,* 19(2), pp.173–193.

Trevarthen, C. (2011b) 'What is it like to be a person who knows nothing? Defining the active intersubjective mind of a newborn human being', *Infant and Child Development,* 20(1), pp.119–135.

Trevarthen, C. and Aitken, K. (2001) 'Infant intersubjectivity, research, theory, and clinical applications', *Journal of Child Psychological Psychiatry,* 42(1), pp.3–48.

Tronick, E. (1998) 'Dyadically expanded states of consciousness and the process of therapeutic change', *Infant Mental Health Journal,* 19(3), pp.290–299.

Tucker, R. (2011) 'How healthy eating advice may have contributed to the obesity epidemic', *The Pharmaceutical Journal,* 1(286), pp.23–30.

UNCRC (1989) *Convention on the Rights of the Child.* Available from: http://www.unicef.org.uk/Documents/Publication-pdfs/UNCRC_PRESS200910web.pdf (Accessed 12 January 2015).

United Nations (2014) *The Millenium Development Goals Report 2014.* Available from: http://www.undp.org/mdg/ (Accessed 4 December 2014).

UNESCO (2005) *UNESCO and Sustainable Development.* Paris: UNESCO. Available at: http://www.google.co.uk/url?sa=t&rct=j&q=&esrc=s&source=web&cd=1&

ved=0CCYQFjAA&url=http%3A%2F%2Funesdoc.unesco.org%2Fimages%2F00
13%2F001393%2F139369e.pdf&ei=npm_VIK2MM2yadmLgrAN&usg=AFQjCNE
rkfVO11gVqYfbPE9N_RxTuZI_RQ (Accessed 10 December 2014).

UNICEF (United Nations International Emergency Children's Fund) (2013a).
*Child well-being in rich countries: A comparative overview.* Innocenti Report
Card 11. UNICEF Innocenti Research Centre.

UNICEF (2013b) *Early Childhood Development.* Available at: http://www.unicef.
org/earlychildhood/ (Accessed 15 December 2014).

UNICEF (2014a) *Children of the Recession: The impact of the economic crisis
on child well-being in rich countries.* Innocenti Report Card 12. UNICEF:
Innocenti Research Centre.

UNICEF (2014b) *United Nations Convention on the Rights of the Child
1989.* Available at: http://www.unicef.org.uk/UNICEFs-Work/UN-Convention/
(Accessed 27 November 2014).

Underdown, A. (2007) *Young Children's Health and Well-being.* Maidenhead:
Open University Press.

Vickery, A. (ed.) (2014) *Developing Active Learning in the Primary Classroom.*
London: Sage.

Vygotsky, L. (1978) *Mind in Society: The Development of Higher Mental Processes.*
Cambridge MA: Harvard University Press.

Walker, P. and John, M. (2012) *From Public Health to Wellbeing: The new driver
for policy and action.* London: Palgrave Macmillan.

Watson, J. (1996) 'The social biofeedback model of parent-affect mirroring',
*International Journal of Psycho-Analysis,* 77, pp.1181–1212.

Watts, A. (2013) *Outdoor Learning through the Seasons: An essential guide for the
early years.* Abingdon: Routledge.

Weare, K. and Gray, G. (2003*) What Works in Developing Children's Emotional
and Social Competence and Wellbeing?* Available at: https://www.google.
co.uk/?gws_rd=ssl#q=weare+and+gray+2003 (Accessed 6 November 2014).

Webster-Stratton, C. and Reid, M. (2004) 'Strengthening Social and Emotional
Competence in Young Children – The Foundation for Early School Readiness
and Success', *Infants and Young Children,* 17(2), pp.96–113.

Whitebread, D. and Bingham, S. (2012) *School Readiness; a critical review of
perspectives and evidence, Occasional Paper no. 2.* London: TACTYC.

WHO (World Health Organisation) (1948) *WHO definition of Health.* Available at:
http://www.who.int/about/definition/en/print.html (Accessed 27 December 2014).

WHO (1984) *Health promotion: a discussion document.* Available at: http://www.
med.uottawa.ca/SIM/data/Health_Definitions_e.htm (Accessed 27 December
2014).

WHO (2014) *10 facts about early child development as a social determinant of
health.* Available at: http://www.who.int/maternal_child_adolescent/topics/
child/development/10facts/en/ (Accessed 7 December 2014).

Winnicott, D. (1971) *Playing and Reality.* London: Routledge.

Winnicott, D. (1973) *The Child, the Family and the Outside World.* London:
Penguin Books.

Woltering, S. and Lewis, M. (2009) 'Developmental pathways of emotional regulation in childhood, a neuropsychological perspective', *Mind, Brain and Education*, 3(3), pp.160–169.

Wood, D., Bruner, J and Ross, G. (1976) 'The role of tutoring in problem-solving', *Journal of Child Psychology and Psychiatry*, 17, pp.89–100.

Wood, K. (2011) *Education: The basics*. Abingdon: Routledge.

Wood, E. and Attfield, J. (2005) *Play, Learning and the Early Childhood Curriculum*. London: Paul Chapman.

Zambo, D. (2008) 'Childcare workers' knowledge about the brain and developmentally appropriate practice', *Early Childhood Education Journal*, 35, pp.571–577.

# INDEX